MONEY MACHINE

By **T.J. Rohleder**
(a.k.a. "The Blue Jeans Millionaire")

Other Great Titles from T.J. Rohleder:

Ruthless Marketing Secrets (Series)
The 2-Step Marketing Secret That Never Fails
Stealth Marketing
The Power of Hype
3 Steps to Instant Profits
Instant Cash Flow
The Blue Jeans Millionaire
How to Turn Your Kitchen or Spare Bedroom into a Cash Machine
The Black Book of Marketing Secrets (Series)
The Ultimate Wealth-Maker
Four Magical Secrets to Building a Fabulous Fortune
The Ruthless Marketing Attack
How to Get Super Rich in the Opportunity Market
$60,000.00 in 90 Days
How to Start Your Own Million Dollar Business
Fast Track to Riches
Five Secrets That Will Triple Your Profits
Ruthless Copywriting Strategies
25 Direct Mail Success Secrets That Can Make You Rich
Ruthless Marketing
24 Simple and Easy Ways to Get Rich Quick
How to Create a Hot Selling Internet Product in One Day
50 in 50
Secrets of the Blue Jeans Millionaire
Shortcut Secrets to Creating High-Profit Products
Foolproof Secrets of Sucessful Millionaires
How to Make Millions While Sitting on Your Ass
500 Ways to Get More People to Give You More Money

FIRST EDITION

ISBN 1-933356-96-0

TABLE OF CONTENTS

Introduction:

By T.J. Rohleder

THANK YOU for buying my book. As you'll see, this was a very wise decision on your part because I'm going to reveal the secret that lets you **turn your entire business into a HUGE MONEY MACHINE that cranks out large amounts of cash and profits every day!**

Does that sound too good to be true?

YOU BET IT DOES!

And yet, this IS TRUE!

So keep an OPEN MIND and I'll lay out the basic secret right now. Are you ready? OKAY, here we go. It starts with the fact that there are ONLY 3 WAYS to build your business: **#1:** you can get more new customers. **#2:** You can sell more higher-ticket items to your current customers. Or **#3:** You can sell MORE OFTEN to your current customers. That's it. The only FOURTH WAY you can build your business is to BUILD A COMPLETE MARKETING SYSTEM that lets you do ALL THREE of these things... Automatically.

And that's the secret you can use to turn your business into A MONEY MACHINE that cranks out large amounts of cash and profits every single day!

Yes, as you'll see, when you go over Chapter One of this book, the secret of the 'MONEY-MACHINE' is to develop a systematic marketing system that lets you find, get, keep, and DO MORE BUSINESS with the very best customers and Clients in your marketplace. It's as simple as that—NOT EASY—and yet, it is very simple.

Just go over Chapter One of this book and you'll discover some of the CORE SECRETS that make it easier for you to do this. Again, building a reliable automatic marketing system is NOT an easy thing to do and, yet, that's THE MAIN REASON WHY you'll NEVER have to worry about any of your competitors ever doing something like this! So take comfort in that. And remember the words of the Greek ship building billionaire, Aristotle Onassis, "The secret to SUCCEEDING BIG in business is to know something that NOBODY ELSE knows." Mr. Onassis was right—and **this 'MONEY MACHINE' secret is something that NONE of your competitors will ever figure out!** By doing what they are unwilling to do, you can DOMINATE YOUR MARKET and get all the money that would normally be going to all of your biggest competitors. So with all that in mind...

Here's What You'll Discover In This Book

This book gives you some of my most powerful marketing secrets, starting with the 'MONEY MACHINE' strategy in Chapter One. Many of the tips, tricks, and strategies I have to teach you sound like common sense and, yet, they truly are secrets because not 1 in 1,000 people know about them and for those who do, FEWER are using them effectively. These secrets... combined together... give you a MAJOR ADVANTAGE over all of the other companies who are competing for the same customers and clients that you are searching for. Just study each chapter carefully and let my greatest marketing secrets be your ultimate secrets to getting all the business that could and should be yours!

And to reward you for purchasing this book, I have...

A great FREE business-building gift for you!

Yes, I have a gift waiting for you that can DRAMATICALLY INCREASE YOUR SALES AND PROFITS! Here's what it's all about: I spent TEN FULL YEARS writing down all of the greatest marketing and success secrets I discovered during that time period. Each day, I took a few notes and, at the end of a decade, I had a GIANT LIST of 6,159 powerful secrets! This list is ALMOST 1,000 PAGES of hardcore money-making ideas and strategies!** **Best of all, this massive collection is now YOURS ABSOLUTELY FREE!** Just go to: www.6159FreeSecrets.com and get it NOW! As you'll see, this complete collection of 6,159 of my greatest marketing and success secrets, far more valuable than those you can buy from others for $495 to $997, is absolutely **FREE.** No cost, no obligation.

Why am I giving away this GIANT COLLECTION of secrets, that took ONE DECADE to discover and compile, FOR FREE? That's simple: I believe many of the people who receive these 6,159 secrets in this huge 955 page PDF document will want to obtain some of our other books and audio programs and participate in our special COACHING PROGRAMS. However, you are NOT obligated to buy anything—now or ever.

I know you're serious about making more money or you wouldn't be reading this. So go to: www.6159FreeSecrets.com and get this complete collection of 6,159 of my greatest marketing and success secrets right now! **You'll get this GREAT FREE GIFT in the next few minutes, just for letting me add you to my Client mailing list,** and I'll stay in CLOSE TOUCH with you... and do all I can to help you make even more money with my proven marketing strategies and methods.

So with all this said, let's begin…

** WARNING: This complete collection of 6,159 marketing and success secrets contains MANY CONTROVERSIAL ideas and methods. Also, it was originally written for MY EYES ONLY and for a few VERY CLOSE FRIENDS. Therefore, the language is X-RATED in some places [I got VERY EXCITED when I wrote many of these ideas and used VERY FOUL LANGUAGE to get my ideas across!] so 'IF' you are EASILY OFFENDED or do NOT want to read anything OFFENSIVE, then please do both of us a favor and DO NOT go to my website and download this FREE gift. THANK YOU for your understanding.

CHAPTER ONE

Most business owners have **no** systematic marketing strategy for getting and keeping customers.

They do everything they can think of — and some of what they're doing is working... But most have never thought deeply about the processes — and methods for:

1. Attracting new customers.

2. Selling them for the largest profit.

3. And then re-selling them as often as possible — for the maximum profits.

All of their marketing activities are hit and miss... They never quantify what is working the best. And, without this quantification — they can never combine the best methods into any kind of reliable automatic marketing system.

Systematic Marketing

Most business owners have no systematic marketing strategy for acquiring and keeping customers. If they do have such a strategy, it's weak. They do everything they can think of, and sure, some of what they're doing works; but most have never thought deeply about the methods required for accomplishing the three things you absolutely have to do to build a business. **First, you've got to attract the very best prospects: customers who've never brought from you before.** They're in your marketplace right now; you just have to get them to do business with you the first time. **Then you have to resell to them for the largest possible profit—as often as possible, and for the maximum margin.**

Most business owners just don't have a good system for doing this. Most or all of their marketing activities are hit and miss, and they never quantify what's working best. Without such quantification, they can never combine the best methods into any kind of a reliable automatic marketing system. *That's* **your goal: a marketing system that works like a well-oiled machine that attracts all of the best new prospects, turns them into first-time buyers, and then does business with them again and again for the largest possible profit.** Now, the machine still has to be constantly tinkered with; it's a very sensitive contraption, not like a car that can go 100,000 miles without a tune-up. It requires care and feeding and fine-tuning and tweaking.

Your goal is to find out what works the best and then convert it into an automatic process, and none of this is easy... even when it's simple. It starts with knowing your customers at an intimate level. That's part of the whole relationship factor I discussed earlier. Who are all these people in your marketplace? What do they really want? What gets their attention? What are they biting on right now? **The more you know and understand that, the easier it is to create what I call a "wow factor."**

We're doing it right now for a new business we're struggling with. We're in the process of putting all this together. It's a new market for us, and quite frankly, it's been a humbling experience for me—because it's going to take us a while to figure all this out. It makes me appreciate our parent company a lot more, because there, we already have a lot of these things figured out. In the new business, it's going to take us maybe six months before we can really implement one of these "wow factors" the way we want to.

We're in the process of arranging to give away something for free, something we know our market really wants. **We had a really good idea, so we developed it in that direction; and now we're going to be able to give it away for free, with certain conditions attached.** It's something that other people are charging money for. If we can successfully do this, we're going to wow a lot of folks... and sure, there are a lot of ifs involved, so we don't know if we can. **We're thinking outside the box.** But if it works... well, it will have a "wow factor" that just blows people away. It will get them so excited they're just going to go crazy. They're going to have to do a double take, because they're not even going to believe what they're seeing.

That's one way we're going to be able to attract the largest number of the very best prospective buyers in this brand new business of ours. Then we've got to sell them things for the highest profit. We've already built that into our business. It's a little different than with most traditional businesses in this market, and we're looking for a few more big-ticket items. We were focused on that from Day One. **One way to do this is add some kind of hot service to your product mix.** A lot of products these days are commodity- based; people can buy them from you or they can get them on the Internet, often for ridiculously cheap prices. **The one way you can be competitive is to offer special services in addition to those products, so you can bump your profit margin up. Or, you can strive to develop something that nobody else has.**

Chris Lakey came up with a brilliant idea one morning as we were brainstorming on this brand new business of ours—an outside-the-box idea that nobody else is doing. It may not work... but we'll never know until we try it. **And again, you really do have to believe it before you see it; you have to step out there on faith, trying to do things that nobody else is doing.**

Think about how to just blow people's minds—and test a lot of different ideas. You're never going to know what works best until you test. Now, I absolutely, positively hate to test. It requires time and patience, and a lot of thinking things through, which I don't like to do. You have to really focus tightly on the details. **Yet testing is the only way you can really get an answer about what works and what doesn't.** The more you test, the more answers you're going to have. The more answers you have, the more often you're going to stumble onto something really, really hot.

You see, most new ideas don't make it. I'm not trying to throw a wet blanket on your enthusiasm, or otherwise be negative; it's just that most new ideas for products, services and business models simply don't work when tested in the marketplace. And if they do work, they usually don't work as well as you want them to. **So you have to test a whole bunch of different ideas in order to find that small percentage that are going to be breakouts.** The more you think outside the box, the more you think about what your customers really want and how to blow their minds, the more you'll succeed. You need to look for ways to give them that "wow factor." **The more you can separate yourself from everybody else, the more good ideas you're going to stumble on.** You're going to kind of get lucky sometimes; you don't know what works the best. Nobody does. **Sometimes, your best route is to spy on your competitors and find out what they're doing — and whenever they find something hot, you just latch on to it, steal the idea, make it yours, and make it better.**

Remember: the real profit comes from getting people to come back repeatedly. Customers go where they're invited, and they stay where they're appreciated — so you've got to re-invite them again and again, and you always need to have something new for them. Now, there's a verse in the Old Testament Book of Ecclesiastics that claims, "There's nothing new under the sun." Maybe that's true in a general way — **but you've got to keep coming up with stuff that sounds new,**

sounds exciting, sounds different. There's got to be a reason for communicating with people, trying to get them to come back. It relates back to that relationship model we talked about in an earlier principle.

The more you can do all this, the more you can systematize your findings into the best possible strategy. Unfortunately, it can't work this way all the time; but you'll have periods of time when it all *does* work, when you get the right offer out to the right group of people (both new customers and established ones) and you've got the thing that brings them back—when you've got something that's really hot. Those will be those magic moments in your business, and we've experienced them here at M.O.R.E., Inc. It's like being on a bicycle, when you're going down a mild hill on a beautiful day, where there's no wind blowing, and you can just throw your arms up in the air. You don't have to pedal; you can just slide down that hill, enjoying every minute.

When these moments happen, savor them, because they won't last. But you *will* have those moments, if you follow what I'm teaching—and those are moments that most business owners will never have. That's because a good 95 percent of business owners (at least) have never really thought about bringing in customers and reselling to them consistently as a specific marketing strategy. I think that most business owners have an idea for a product or a service, or have something they're good at, and they turn that into a business. Maybe they run some ads or have a listing in the Yellow Pages, and that's about it. **They don't think about a systematic approach to acquiring and retaining customers. But that's the way a marketer thinks.**

And therein, I think, lies the biggest problem with trying to get people to shift how they think about their businesses. **Most people are good at doing whatever it is they do;** they may be good at being an electrician, a hairstylist, a consultant of some kind, or whatever... but that's about the extent of it. **When it comes to promoting their business and thinking about their business from a marketing standpoint, they don't have a clue.** That's not to fault them; that's just the way it is.

The way you put together a systematic marketing strategy is, **first of all, to become aware that you need one.** Only then can you start constructing it. This can be very challenging, and the specifics will depend on what your business model is and how much profit margin you have with whatever you sell. **You'll need to track your overhead, how much you're clearing on each transaction, and how many transactions you need to break even.** There are all kinds of things that go into the way a specific business operates. But the system has to be there, no matter what shape or size it takes. **You have to have something that attracts new customers and gets them to buy the first time, then gets them to re-buy repeatedly for the maximum profit each time, so that you can build a viable, long-term business.**

Most businesses don't do any kind of specific targeted direct marketing beyond their Yellow Pages listing and ads in the newspaper; maybe they're even advertising in multiple newspapers. They might have ads on television. They might, occasionally, be sponsoring an activity in town; maybe they've got a sports team in the local bitty basketball league or the local baseball little league. Maybe every Saturday the kids are out there playing soccer, and they've got their company's name on the back of all the jerseys, doing some advertising that way.

All these things are happening, but none of it's being thought about as part of a marketing system. **They're just throwing a bunch of stuff against the wall and seeing what sticks, hoping that enough does to generate a profit so they can keep their doors open.** That's hardly the best way to approach things, so if that's your method, you need to accept the fact that it's *not* the best approach, and start to shift the way you think about bringing in customers into your business. **With a little work, you can at least begin to turn the corner and start to figure some of this out.**

Again, it's not always easy; in fact, it can be a real struggle at times. But being aware of the problem is the first step toward fixing it. **Just change the way you think about your marketing, and make an attempt to account for every dollar you spend in promoting your business.** In other words, when you start running your ads, they need to have some kind of response mechanism attached. Whenever someone comes into your door, or when they call, you have to be able to at least attempt to find out where they came from. Now, there are a couple of problems when you do that. Sometimes they don't remember which ad they saw, which is an issue when your ads are all over the place. Sometimes, your sales clerk might not be as aggressive as they should be in asking. Maybe they forget once in a while; it's not foolproof.

But in general, you should make an effort to get some kind of system in place so you can begin getting an idea of where your marketing is working and where it isn't. In doing so, you start to develop the ability to keep track of which ads are worth investing more money in and which are better off trashed. **That's why everything you do needs to be trackable somehow**—whether it's a coupon to get them in the store, or a radio commercial, or a kid's baseball jersey. There are any number of things you can do to identify the specific advertisement, so you can monitor which ads are effective at bringing in customers. **Because, of course, you want to spend more money doing things that work, and less money doing things that don't.**

Once you can determine where they're coming from, and where to invest more heavily in advertising, you have to start pushing to make the largest possible profit while re-selling to them again and again. That's part of simple database marketing. **One of the things we always recommend is that you build a mailing list somehow, and you can do this simply enough by offering some kind of gift.** I've talked about our new pet boutique business, and how we're offering to give away something that we think all the people in that marketplace are interested in. All they have to do is sign up for our rewards program. Through that, we capture the contact information of as many people as possible. Not everybody who comes in the store is signing up, so we're not capturing *everybody's* contact information. **But ideally, over time, we'll build a substantial database of people that we can build relationships with.**

Those relationships we build will turn into the platform from which we make future sales. For example, we can invite people back to our store for special events; **having that list puts us in the position of being able to communicate with our**

customers at will, which is a necessity if you want to resell to someone repeatedly. If you don't capture their contact information, how do you get in touch with your best customers to let them know about opportunities to do more business with you? Oh, they may see the occasional ad in the newspaper, but that's not personal at all. There's nothing like a direct response mechanism to attract attention.

Now, you might say, "But direct mail is expensive. I've heard it costs a lot of money." **That's true, but you don't have to use mail if you don't want to.** You can try e-mail, though it's likely to get stuck in the spam folder or bumped down the list of important things to read. And it's easy to hit that delete button, so be cautious. **Provide something of value to them that makes them to want to read it, and maybe you'll have a better open rate for your email.**

You see? You don't have to spend a lot of money. Maybe you're just sending postcards out, inviting people to come into the store for special events; but whatever it is, **you have to have some way to communicate with them, because there is *nothing* like a direct selling message to get people to come back and do more business with you.** Without that system of attracting customers and then reselling to them, you're just randomly hoping that something sticks. You're going with a haphazard approach, not knowing what really works. You're throwing a lot of money away by chasing after bad advertising that's not producing the results you need.

Again, directed communication like this is not foolproof; nor is it easy. There are a lot of details to work out, specifically as it relates to your business. In fact, with our new business, we're going through a transition period right now in regards to this strategy. We believe wholeheartedly in the approach, and in the idea that you need a systematic marketing strategy; but it really is difficult in the beginning. There are challenges there, especially when things that don't go right. **There are definitely frustrations... but getting the system in place will provide lifelong profits and a solid foundation for the success of your business.** The sooner you can get that nailed down, the better off you're going to be.

Our parent company has been in business for over 20 years, and during that time, we've perfected a system for using this strategy in our business. **We've had plenty of failures and successes as we worked that method out, and we've reached the point where we've got our system down strong.** Our new business, this other company, not so much. The system is in its infancy; at this writing, the store has been open less than a month, so we're still trying to figure it out. Hopefully, we'll look back on this business 10 or 20 years from now and say, "Remember when we struggled to try to find the identity of our marketing system, back in the very beginning?" and we'll be able to laugh it off and say, "Look where we are now!" Right now, we're just not there. We're struggling with exactly how to put together what the system looks like for this new business.

Every business is different, so you have to find the identity of this system within your business. Find the best systematic strategy for attracting customers, and then reselling to them often as possible. Once you have that system in place, it can work like magic, cranking out the cash on demand just like an ATM machine. **Any time you want cash, you crank up the**

system. You just keep it going, keep feeding it with the advertising that you're doing that you *know* works, and the rest, as they say, is history.

Yet most business owners never figure this out, because they're unwilling to go through the pain, the confusion, and the frustration. I have to say, I never realized just how good we've got it with our parent company until we tried something new! It gives me a whole new appreciation for all those other business owners struggling right now, because it's tough. **It's *very* tough, and that's why most people never get to that place where it becomes easy. They're not willing to keep pushing through the pain.**

Here's a great quote that I used to have posted on my wall: **"Wisdom through suffering. You only get smart by going through the pain." That's the *only* way you do it.** If you want a great body, you've got to go put yourself through pain in the gym every day. You've got to tear yourself down before you can build yourself up physically. Well, the same thing is true for other aspects of life, including business. **Those who do more get more; those who do less get less. That's life.**

CHAPTER TWO

Spend more money to make more money:

✓ "In direct marketing <u>it's the cost to get the sale</u> — not to make a mailing (or series of mailings) that counts." — *Jon Goldman*

✓ Many times, the secret is to spend more money, <u>not less</u>. This is especially true when you are making offers to your best prospects and customers.

Spend More Money
to Make More Money

You often have to spend more money to make more money. This isn't always the case, of course, but you do have to *willing* to do it. In direct marketing, the most important thing is the cost required to get the sale. **Often it takes a lot of money to get that sale, and you have to be constantly aware of this reality; you have to go into it with your eyes wide open.** So many people don't, and I'll explain why in a moment.

It's especially necessary to spend more money when you're making offers to your best prospects or customers. Ultimately, it's all about dollars spent versus dollars made. Business really is the simplest thing on earth, when you get right down to it. I get so upset whenever I go to the bookstore and visit the business section. I'll browse the books on marketing and sales, and inevitably, I'll see that they're complicating it unnecessarily. They're doing it because it's self-serving for them to do so... and the truth is, a lot of the books on business are written by people who've never really been in business for themselves. They've always worked for Fortune 1000 or Fortune 5000 companies; they don't understand a thing about small business.

It really bothers me whenever I see all these complicated books written by consultants who want to show off and make things complicated, so they can line their pockets—because when people read those books, they get confused about what to do. **All these books do is turn people away from the joy of being self-employed.** And it *is* a tremendous joy, because business really is very simple! Now, it's not always easy; please don't misunderstand me here. In fact, the more money you want to make, the more difficult it becomes. But the root of it, the basic components of it, are simple enough.

That said, we're living in a vastly over-competitive, overcrowded marketplace. The best, most lucrative markets are already inhabited by some extremely sharp marketers, companies and individuals with deep pockets, and there are a lot of confusing messages out there for the prospective buyer. **That's one of the reasons you've got to spend more money to make more money, because it takes more selling power to reach the best prospects.** And yet most people are trying to do it the exact opposite! Most marketers are doing what P.T. Barnum—truly one of the greatest marketers who ever lived—characterized as trying to catch a whale by using a minnow as bait.

While that metaphor's a little outdated, the concept behind it is as true now as it was 150 years ago. **Most people want instant, impressive results, but they don't want to invest the effort and money necessary to get those results.** You'll see that mistake rear its ugly head in the fact that people just want to run small ads, or they want to mail out little, tiny postcards, and then they expect all the money in the world to just come rushing in. It never happens. Selling is a process. Marketing is a process. If you want more, you've got to be willing to do and spend more. **Each sale that you make has to be bought.**

In fact, all of us are really in the business of buying sales at a profit. I want you to think about that; I was in the business for eight years before I really latched onto that concept. **Now, once you *do* wrap your arms around that concept, you'll see that buying sales means you have to spend some money.** The people who are willing to spend more are the ones who do a more effective job of selling—and it's all about salesmanship. That's what *all* marketing is about: selling stuff. When you spend more money, you're able to separate yourself from all those competitors who are screaming and shouting and trying to get the attention of the same prospects you're trying to attract. You have to do things that prove your case to people. **You have to prove why what you have to offer is worth far more than the money you're asking them to give you in return.**

In a direct-mail situation, we like to say that you have to kill some trees, in that you need to write some long-form sales letters to be truly effective. Some of our sales letters are as much as 40 or 50 pages long. **Why? Because we're proving our case to people.** Anybody can *say* that they've got something that's the greatest thing since sliced pizza, but you've got to prove it to your prospects. They're so skeptical it's not even funny, and for good reason. Therefore, you spend more money so you can build trust, so you can establish value, so you can tell your entire marketing story, and most importantly of all, so that you can wear down their resistance. You see, the best prospects out there really want to buy what you're selling, assuming that you've qualified them properly. **But they've got all this sales resistance to overcome, and it's impossible to wear that sales resistance down if you're trying to do it on the cheap.**

And yet that's what so many marketers are trying to do; they want to mail a few postcards, or do it all on the Internet. They want to live in a fantasy world where everybody believes every word they say, where people magically have all this extra money to spend, where there's an absence of all these hard core, razor-sharp, ambitious, and aggressive marketers who are all trying to go after the same business. Like all fantasy worlds, it's not real; the reality *never* lives up to that fantasy. The reality is that people are more skeptical than ever, there's more competition than ever, and some of those competitors are really, really good at what they do. **The average prospect doesn't know who to believe anymore. They don't really trust anybody, so you've got to be willing to spend the money to make that sale.**

Now, one of the techniques that we use again and again at M.O.R.E., Inc. is **two-step marketing.** This has made us millions of dollars, and it can make *you* millions of dollars. Basically, here's how it works: you go ahead and run those small ads or you mail those postcards, doing things to separate the smaller group of qualified prospective buyers from the bigger group. That's step number one. You can still run all those dirt cheap ads and do all that inexpensive Internet stuff. **You're casting your net out there, telling them just enough to attract their attention, to get them to raise their hand and take an initial action.** Once you've separated them out that way, you know they're qualified as a prospect. You may have to do more and more things to qualify them. **Once you have— once you know they're interested in what you have to say and what you're offering—you can go out and spend a lot of money to do a very complete job of stating your case,** proving that what you're saying is true, building trust with those people, wearing down that sales resistance, and then getting their money.

In fact, you'll get the money that other people *aren't* getting. There's a lot of money left on the table that all these other marketers are losing, because they're just teasing these people, not doing an effective job of selling. Now, in some cases, what adds fuel to these marketers' delusion is that they may get a few sales—and they may all of a sudden start patting themselves on the back. They may start feeling 10 foot tall and bulletproof, because they spent a little money and actually made some money. **But the question is, How much *more* money could they have made if they were willing to properly use this principle of spending more money to make more money?**

I'm talking about spending more money intelligently, you see. In the world of direct response marketing, you can spend an enormous sum per prospect in order to "break the sale" or "break it," as we like to say: that is, to convert those leads into sales. **You can do that even as you test things on a small basis.** Let's say you're spending $50 to generate the lead and then do everything possible to close that sale. Well, if you're just testing to a small group of maybe 10 prospects, $50 each isn't so much. It's only going to cost you $500 total, so you're intelligently using your money.

I'm not talking about gambling here, or spending recklessly, or doing stupid things like the government does every day of the week. We're talking about business here:

making a profit, where you can then test those more expensive things to prove beyond any shadow of a doubt that the extra money that you're spending is worth it, that there's no guesswork here. It's all done in a way that makes you the most profit possible.

Here's a quick example: as I write this, one week from today we're going to send 4,000 pieces of mail to our best customers. Each of those pieces is going to consist of the same 32-page sales letter that I'm finishing up right now. Two thousand of those letters will have a dollar bill attached to them, and 2,000 won't. We're using security envelopes, and we're personalizing all the pieces inside, and the only other difference is that half will have a brand new, crisp one dollar bill attached to the letter. There are extra labor costs for us to attach those dollar bills, some extra security measures that we have to take on, and then, of course, there are the bills themselves. Also, all of them go into a nice security bag, a really fancy plastic bag that separates itself from everything else our customers are getting in the mail. Those cost us a quarter each, but they're going to make the prospects stand up and take notice.

The idea is to prove, once and for all, whether the dollar is well spent or not. If the dollar proves itself, then we'll test a two-dollar bill or a five-dollar bill against a dollar bill. And we'll prove that one outperforms the other. **It's not about what something costs that matters; it's about what it makes you, and this is all about salesmanship.** If I had to describe the best salespeople in one word, it would be *relentless.* They simply don't give up. They're like those little bulldogs that grab ahold of your pant leg and just won't let go. They refuse to quit. **They**

stay after the prospect over and over. They either drive people crazy or drive them to buy. You've got to duplicate that principle of selling in all of your marketing. **You do that by using this principle of spending more money to make more money.**

Unfortunately, a lot of business people, especially those new to the game, are suffering under the delusion that sales are going to be easily had—that you can just tell people you have a product and people will want to buy it, even if they aren't interested in it. As a result, there's this belief that you have to try to be as frugal in your marketing as possible—especially in times like those prevailing as I write this, when the economy isn't doing so great. When times are tough, people instantly go into this frugal mode, doing without services they enjoyed in times of prosperity. They hunker down, they slow down, they kind of shut down. It affects all parts of a business, including marketing... and if you're not careful, it will hurt your ability to make sales.

So they might cut back on some of their services; they switch their cell phone to a cheaper plan, or limit long distance calls, or go to a slower Internet speed. Or they might try to consume less energy, so their electric bill is lower. They might try to conserve paper. And those aren't necessarily bad things. **But when it comes to marketing, when it comes to selling, you have to be very careful not to over-economize.** It's not unusual to see businesses shut down or scale way back on their marketing. They'll run fewer and/or smaller ads, stop advertising on TV, try to make their mailings cheaper somehow.

Whatever the marketing method is, the concept is the same.

People tend to scale back whatever they're doing. **Now, maybe when times are lean, you do look at testing differently and reconsider how you take risks with your marketing, and again, that's not necessarily a bad thing.** When times are good and you've got a great cash flow, you're more willing to take chances on marketing, throwing a few experiments in with the tried-and-true advertising you do on a regular basis, stuff that you know gets you the results you need. **When times are lean, you focus on what you *know* produces the best results.**

But that doesn't necessarily mean that you cut back on your marketing; it just means you're more strategic. Strategy doesn't necessarily mean spending less money. It may mean spending less money in some areas, or avoiding the riskier kinds of marketing. But the lean times are when you have to become more aggressive with your core advertising: direct mail, magazine advertising, TV ads, or whatever you consider basic. **You've got to make something work, and spending more money to make more money is one of the ways you get there.**

Of course, you still have to watch your numbers, and let them tell you what to do. **But, in general, with direct response marketing especially, the ultimate cost to get the sale is what counts.** That's what you need to pay attention to. Is there a profit, or not? If you have a $1,000 offer and it takes you $750 to make that sale, can you make a profit at that? Of course; you made a $250 profit. But is that enough to let you keep your doors open and pay your employees, pay yourself nicely, pay for your overhead and all your other costs of doing business, and still have money left over at the end? If the answer is yes, then you're good. If the answer is no, then maybe you need to find a way to make more of those $1,000 sales—or maybe your base cost should be $1,500 instead of $1,000.

The key is to not be afraid to spend money to make more money. Usually, scaling back results in fewer sales, whereas more aggressive marketing results in more sales. **If you cut back on your marketing, you're probably going to starve your business of the cash flow you need to survive.** Rather than do that, you need to bring more money into your business: by selling harder, by doing a better, more aggressive job of attracting new customers, and by doing more business with your existing customers.

Here's something that's a bit off the subject, but still related; and I think we can all learn from this. I've been thinking about taxes lately. There's a philosophy in economics that says that there's a line in taxation beyond which the government will see revenues decline. If they raise taxes too high, then yes, technically they're bringing in more money; but the problem is that soon, there's no economic activity to produce those taxes. If people are taxed too much, they'll stop doing the things that generate the tax revenue. For example, this is why a lot of people argue against cigarette taxes. The government thinks that if you tax cigarettes, you're going to raise a lot of money, because there are so many smokers. But the thing they forget is that every time you raise taxes on cigarettes, more people quit smoking. Therefore, the government loses the tax revenue they had when taxes were lower.

On the other side of that equation, if you tax something at a lower rate, the activity continues and the government gets more money. Now, obviously, if the tax rate is zero, the government gets nothing. If you tax people at 100%, there's going to be no incentive to do anything, and so the government also gets zero. **So where's the happy medium—the point where you don't discourage the activity, but you still maximize the income?** Where is that line that you can't cross, but that you want to toe to make sure you get the highest possible cut?

Those of us in business have to use the same philosophy. **How much money should you spend to maximize your profits?** You have to experiment constantly to find that line. **Sadly, most people are in a position where they aren't spending enough; and by not spending enough, their sales aren't high enough.** They're not making as much profit as they should be. On the other hand, it's easy to go too far—where you're overspending yourself into no profitability. **It's never obvious where that line is, but I'll tell you this: it's probably higher than you're comfortable with.** Even so, don't be afraid to spend money to make money. Generally speaking, the more you're willing to spend on your marketing, the more money will move through your business to provide you with an income to pay employees, to pay your overhead, and to pay your taxes. **All that money will be there if you find the right balance of spending more money to make more money.**

That's where the power lies—and I have to admit that you have to do things the right way for this to work, especially in terms of being logical in how you spend the money and, frankly, in holding onto the reins of spending yourself. Because you *can* just abdicate all your marketing to somebody else, let them spend a lot of money, and just lose it to no effect. **So you've got**

to constantly have your fingers on the pulse of your business; you've constantly got to be watching your numbers, and letting them tell you what to do. All this has to be done intelligently. There's no excuse for stupidity here.

If you're proactive, and you spend the money intelligently on your best prospects, you almost can't spend enough—assuming all your other numbers, like the ticket price and profit margins, are set properly. For every reckless entrepreneur who spends more money and goes broke, there must be thousands who aren't spending enough.

Our friend Bill Glazier has a quote that I want to leave you with before I move on: **"You can't kill an elephant with a BB gun."** It doesn't matter if you have the best BB gun in the world, it won't penetrate that elephant's hide, even if it shoots BBs like a machine gun. At best, you're going to piss that elephant off, and he might stomp you to death. You need heavy ammunition if you're going to try to kill an elephant. You need a massive rifle before you can take one of those monsters down.

And the average prospect is very much like the elephant in this example, in that it takes a lot to bring them down: that is, it takes a lot to make that sale. **As long as you keep thinking like that, then none of the potential difficulties should discourage you.** In fact, you should be encouraged instead, simply because you know that most people don't spend enough. They're leaving a lot of money on the table, and *you're* going to come in there and clean house. You're going to get all that money that could and should be theirs, because you're willing to spend more money to convert all the sales they're abandoning. They're not telling the prospective buyer enough for that person to make an intelligent decision and choose them over all their other potential choices.

This single strategy can potentially make you millions of dollars. It's all about trying to do everything possible to get the highest qualified prospective buyers to raise their hands. Take an initial act, separating that smaller group from the larger group— and then just go after them, and be relentless in your pursuit.

CHAPTER THREE

**Human beings love to repeat
the same behaviors over
and over again.**

**If you can get them to do something
one time — you can get them to
do it the next time.**

Harnessing Repeat Behavior

We human beings love to repeat the same behaviors over and over again. **If you can get someone to do something one time, you can usually get them to do it the next time, too.** Now, I don't want to minimize human complexity; people can be quite complicated indeed, but from an emotional standpoint—at least when it comes to them spending money—they can be very predictable. They keep doing the same things over and over again. That's why this is such a powerful principle!

Almost all behavior is repeat behavior, but this is especially true when it comes to people buying. If you get them to buy once, they'll buy from you again and again. **The trick is to get them to buy that first time.** And you've got to think about this as a process, not an event. **All marketing is a process.** So you get them to take a small step, and as the old clichés goes, one thing really does lead to another. Ultimately, you're trying to get people to take some serious action here; **you want them to become customers for life.** You want to make that high ticket sale to them, too, so you can make as much money as you can from the smallest group of customers. That's asking people to do a lot, especially when we're talking about the overcrowded nature of our marketplace and all the different messages out there. So just focus on a series of discrete steps, and on getting them to take that series of steps that ultimately leads to the big step of them spending a lot of money with you on a regular basis for as long as possible.

Let me tell you a quick, slightly off-color story; don't worry, I'll keep it PG-13 and let your imagination fill in the blanks. I'm not telling you this to be crude or anything like that; it's just that sometimes, the most extreme examples are the best ones. We tend to remember everything extreme. In any case, the late great Gary Halbert, one of the greatest marketers that I personally had a chance to learn from, once told me a story about a strip club. Gary was a colorful individual and liked to go to those places, and there was one particular place in Miami that he claimed had better-looking strippers than any of the other joints he used to go to. The way Gary told the story, these were Sport Illustrated swimsuit models, and they were kind of buff.

So Gary got to know the owner of the strip club, and one day he said to the guy, "How in the world do you do this? How do yet get these gorgeous women to get up on the stage and do this kind thing? Because you know, at most strip clubs, the women aren't nearly this attractive."

And the guy said, "It's real simple. We don't pay them any extra, but they make extra anyway because it's a popular place and lots of people come here. We start them out as cocktail waitresses first, and a lot of these gals even hesitate to take on a cocktail waitress job. **But we pay them three times more money than all the other cocktail waitress jobs, and they sign on board with the stipulation that they will never, ever have to take their clothes off if they don't want to.** And so they sign up. They become cocktail waitresses serving drinks to customers and taking orders for more drinks. After a few months, they get to know the customers, and they find out that most of these

40

people are just sad, lonely, depressed, married men with money.

"As they get to know the customers, they tend to loosen up. They find out it's not such an evil place, and if anything, they start feeling sorry for the customers. Then they meet the women up there on stage and get a chance to know them. **They find out the incredible amounts of money the dancers are making, and it's only a matter of time before a large percentage of those women**—ladies who wouldn't even consider being a cocktail waitress unless I paid them three times the normal rate, and promised them they'd never need to strip—**decide they want to strip after all.** Not all of them, but a percentage of them do get up there." That was the guy's secret.

Now, that may be a bad story to some people. I'm sure that some of you readers might feel uneasy or offended. But I didn't tell the story to offend you; I just want you to remember it. It's an extreme example, which is the reason why it stuck in my brain in the first place. **It perfectly illustrates the principle of getting people to repeat the same behaviors over and over, and then trying to get them to take one small step before you try to get them to take the next small step.**

If this strip club owner had approached those women as strippers, there's no way on God's green Earth that most of them would've agreed to it. They would've just run. Now, let me paint you a picture. **You just can't go to your best prospects and ask them to give you a lot of money until and unless you've done things to win their trust and lower their sales resistance.** Let them get know you, let them get to trust you, and make them comfortable in the process. When people have a lot of sales resistance, they're not comfortable at all. They're leery, they're skeptical, and they just don't trust you. They're afraid you're going to rip them off. They don't believe a single word you say. So if you just go to somebody and try to sell them something expensive right away, they're going to be turned off. **So you build your sales message in a series of steps.** One sale leads to the next, and you stair-step them. You don't try to make your biggest sale right up front; you start slow and stay after people.

Here are a couple of more G-rated metaphors. **Think of the Chinese torture treatment.** (That still may be a little bit extreme, but it's clean at least.) The Chinese torture treatment is just one drop of water on the forehead after another after another after another. Who would ever imagine that a drop of water would drive somebody crazy! What kind of foolish thinking is that? But according to legend, that's exactly what *did* drive people crazy, because hour upon hour upon day after day of these little drops wouldn't let them sleep. They went totally crazy as a result. **A little tiny drop of water actually produced something huge.**

Then there's the diamond cutter analogy. A professional diamond cutter starts with the raw stone, but they've got to bring out the natural cut within that stone. So they examine it very carefully before they even start. Then they use a little tiny hammer and a little tiny chisel, and wield them with a series of very, very tiny taps. If they used a bigger hammer and chisel, it would reduce that stone to dust—valuable diamond dust, but not nearly as valuable as a fine cut in a piece of jewelry. So they use tiny tools, wielded delicately. Each tap might not have an obvious effect; it might be the 217th tiny tap that splits the stone perfectly. **But all the previous taps contributed. It was a**

process, not an event. It's not something you do just once.

As I discussed earlier, everybody wants to spend less money to make more money. They want to do their marketing in a single step. You can't do that! **It's a series of small steps; it's a process.** People have to be introduced to something very slowly, in a small way. You don't start a baby out eating steak; you start him out on mashed apples and strained apricots. Some of that stuff just smells terrible and looks worse, but that's what little babies start eating first. Then, eventually, you give them a little piece of hot dog and maybe a little piece of hamburger. And when they're five or six years old, you can give them their first steak.

You have to do the same thing with business prospects. **You have to string them along slowly, and build that relationship. That's really what it's all about: a relationship.** This is one of the secrets that makes multi-level marketing a billion-dollar enterprise: because people are exploiting their personal relationships. In many cases, those relationships took years to develop and build. If I have a friendship with somebody that goes back 20 or 30 years, I've already won their trust. They like me, they trust me, I'm their friend. So if I say, "Hey, Bill, Look at this business opportunity I have here," Bill is going to listen, because we've been friends for so long. We've eaten a thousand dinners together. We've shared intimate conversation. We've gone to ball games together—whatever. Fill in the blanks. It's a well-developed relationship, so all I have to do is say, "Hey, come to this meeting with me." You come to the meeting, you sign up. **But think about all the things that happened before that: it's a process.**

Chris Lakey, me, and my stepson Chris have a company that we've been running for about six years, and we're getting ready to put a new business model into action. This business model includes all the elements I've been talking about in this chapter, and it all starts with a small step that our prospects have to take. **Our real money is going to come from an ongoing service that we provide to these customers, hopefully, every month for at least a year or two.** But we expect to actually perform this service for them only half-a-dozen times on average. We don't know, at this point, how long we'll be able to maintain those individual relationships with the customers. What we *do* know is that the initial step they take is going to cost under $500. We're keeping that price very low, and we're willing to just break even on that first $500 sale. **We're trading dollars for dollars here. For every dollar we spend on marketing, all we want is a dollar back.**

You don't get rich trading dollars for dollars, right? Wrong. In this case, we plan on getting *very* rich. In fact, I told Chris Lakey this morning that this could end up making us more money than anything else in the past six years, because once somebody spends that $500 with us, that's a gateway. **The real money to be made on this new business comes from all the related items.** And that's a keyword there: *related*. We'll offer them closely-related additional services that are sold, in some cases, on a till-forbid basis. What this means is that we continue to make the sale to them automatically until they tell us to stop. That's how many magazine subscriptions work, for example.

And because the front end is so closely tied to the back end—the "back end" meaning all the additional services we're going to be offering to these people over an extended period of time—**when they spend that first $500, we know we're getting people who are extremely qualified for what we're selling.** They're already sold on the main idea; they're already excited about it. The additional monthly service we're going to try to get people to take on will be a close cousin to what they bought the first time. So as long as we just trade dollars for dollars, we're using the first principle I talked about in a previously: we're buying the sale. **Remember, every sale has to be bought.**

Well, in this case, we're spending $500 to get $500 back. There's no profit whatsoever there; our profit is in the additional revenue from other items. **It's the back end that makes you rich, along with all the repeat business that you do with people over a long period of time.** That's responsible for every fortune that anybody ever makes, except for some extreme exceptions—and they *are* exceptions. **For the most part, the secret to getting rich is to get people to come back again and again, spending more money at a higher profit margin each time.** That's the process, and you have to think it through like that. You begin with the end in mind. In this case, we know that the real gravy is to be made on the back end, selling the additional monthly services to these people. So we're more than happy to buy those sales.

We could never start out by asking these people to give us $3,000, which is what we ultimately want from them. Some of our additional, related services are going to sell for a few grand, though of course we'll have cheaper options as well. And to our market, that's pretty expensive—so we have to realize that reaching this point is a process that takes time. **Therefore we just worry about that first step, which leads to the next, and the next, until we're where we want to be.** We get them to indulge in repeat behavior, which is just human nature in the first place.

This principle is something all marketers have to take notice of, or it will be to their own detriment—because **people are definitely creatures of habit.** The things they do over and over again will either help you in your business or hurt you, depending on whether or not you can capitalize on them. As it relates to marketing, and getting people to become repeat customers, you definitely have to take advantage of this aspect of human behavior.

One example that always comes to mind when I think of this concept is a story about a dry cleaner who had tremendous success. He decided to get some new business by running an ad in the local paper, offering to dry clean for free everything you could fit in a trash bag, for one time only. He had droves of people reply, and he did all their dry cleaning free. Obviously, he lost money on that—it was a cost of doing business. But he followed it up with an offer to do it again for half-price. He sent it to those people who responded the first time, and a percentage of them brought another trash bag full of dry cleaning in, and he did it for them again. Then he did it once more. The point was that **he understood the psychology of human behavior, and that if he could get someone to repeat the same behavior three times, he would have a dry cleaning customer for life.**

People rarely change dry cleaners; a cleaner really has to ruin something and make a horrible impression on you for you to go somewhere else. So if most people visit a dry cleaner three times, that's where they're going to have their dry cleaning done until they move or die... or the dry cleaner goes out of business. **This guy understood that concept, and set about to getting as many people as possible to come to his dry cleaning store three times.** Once he had them that third time, he knew that they would most likely be a customer for life. He was capitalizing on their behavior when it came to dry cleaning.

And I would assume that this applies to all kinds of other service businesses as well. You probably go to the same barber over and over, and you won't bother to change barbers unless he really butchers your hair. For those businesses, the trick, or the strategy, is to figure out how to get customers to repeat the same behavior those three times. If you can get them three times, then you've probably got them for life. **So running special promotions to attract people once may not be enough when you consider this strategy.** You need to have them do business with you three times, on average.

But what can you do to trigger that repeatable behavior multiple times, so you can lock in their business? One way is to follow the strategy outlined earlier: spend more money to make more money. **You've got to be willing to aggressively spend money in order to acquire and retain customers who will do business with you multiple times.** In the case of the dry cleaner, he was willing to spend money by giving away something. A bag full of clothes probably represented a substantial short-term loss for this guy, and yet he was willing to see what most other dry-cleaners *aren't* willing to see: that if he'd just spend money in the short-term, giving away some of his dry cleaning services, by the time he cycled people through three times he'd have customers for life—and that lifetime of profits would more than make up for all the income he'd lost.

So when you're working on your next promotion, remember these two strategies: that it takes money to make money, and that human beings love to repeat the same behavior over and over again. Getting them to do something once, and then getting them to do it a second time and a third time, can be the secret to building a customer base loyal to your business. Barring any major mistakes on your part, those people will be customers for life. **Whenever they need the type of product or service you sell, they'll think of you first.** They'll seek you out, and your advertising becomes even more effective, because you know they already want to do business with you. **They're *trained* to do business with you.**

So find a way to capitalize on this aspect of human behavior. The more sporadic your marketing is, the less targeted and calculated it is, the more likely you'll lose customers. Your customer bucket, the flow of people into your business and out of your business, will have way too many holes. But if you can figure out how to get your customers to take repeatable actions long enough that they become comfortable doing business with you, your bucket will have less holes in it, and the holes will be smaller. You'll find yourself retaining more of your customers, which, in the end, means more profits for you. **It's generally cheaper to sell to existing customers than to get new customers, so you'll find yourself with more profits and a healthier company.**

Let me leave you with one more story, one I've told before;

but I think it bears repeating here, because it's about the insatiability of prospects in some markets, including the one that we've been in since 1988. Less than two years after we started our company, we hired a fellow named Randy Hamilton. He still works with us today, over 20 years later, and Randy's a very smart guy. Well, he took one look at the low-end turnkey business opportunities we sell, and said, "Man, I've got to go get my resume out there. This company's not going to make it. It's not going to be around long. This isn't a long-term business here." He knew a lot about business, and was sure we'd fail.

Then he just got busy and forget that he needed to circulate that resume. We had more work than he could possibly handle; and when he came up for air a few months later, he told himself again, "Man, I've got to get my resume out there. This company's going down." That went on for a couple years... until he just forgot it altogether. **The one thing that Randy didn't understand then, as smart as he is, is the insatiability of our market, which bears directly on this principle: if a prospect buys something once, they'll buy again and again.** We've been developing all kinds of different low-end business opportunities and selling them very successfully, again and again, to many of the same customers, because the customer who buys one business opportunity will buy another one. **They're insatiable; they just can't be satisfied.** In fact, far from satisfying them, a purchase often fuels the fire that leads to more desire that leads to them buying again. Not only does purchasing not satiate their desire, **it *inflames* their desire.** The purchase actually makes them want to purchase more. Think about that.

49

Now, some markets are more insatiable than others. Some markets don't have any insatiability, but those are the ones you want to stay out of. **Look for lucrative markets where people just can't get enough of whatever it is that you're selling, and you** *will* **get rich—as long as you practice the principles I'm teaching you here.**

CHAPTER FOUR

⊙⊙⊙⊙⊙

The secret of a good direct mail letter:

It doesn't shout at people

—

it lures them in.

⊙⊙⊙

The Secret of
a Good Sales Letter

The secret of a good direct mail sales letter is that it doesn't shout at people; it lures them in. This is a very subtle marketing technique, and it's critical that you understand it if you expect to maximize your earnings. So let's start with me helping you understand the premise of *all* direct mail letters—or any direct response marketing, for that matter. It's not really a form of advertising, you see; it's not really even a form of marketing, because marketing is far too general a word for what it does. **Good direct mail is one thing and one thing only: salesmanship.**

Now, a lot of people have different ideas about what it means to sell, and many of those ideas are valid. **But I'll tell you one thing that selling isn't, and that's shouting.** Sure, sometimes you have to be a little loud to get attention—and speaking of attention, when it comes to salesmanship, there's a simple formula you can use. It's not perfect in every detail, but it's more true than not. **We call it the A.I.D.A. formula, where A.I.D.A. is an acronym for Attention, Interest, Desire and Action.**

Professional sales trainers disagree on a lot of things, but I think they would all agree on this simple formula. It's a powerful formula, and you should emulate it with all your direct response marketing. **First you get their Attention; and again, sometimes to you have to be a bit loud, which is why we use**

giant headlines sometimes. You're trying to flag people down—not necessarily shouting at them, but definitely doing something bold to get their attention. **Then you get them Interested, showing them what's in it for them. You tease them a little with the potential benefits, and then inflame their Desire to make them want it even more. And then, finally, you get them to take Action.**

A direct mail letter mirrors this entire process. It pulls people in; that's the Attention part of it. Then it shows them why it's in their best interests to consider whatever it is you're offering, which is the Interest part of it. Next, it does things to whet their appetite, make them want it, proving that what you have is worth more than the money you're asking for in exchange. That's Desire. And finally, it tells them exactly what to do. It commands them to take action; it doesn't leave anything to question. **You have to be very clear with people in the Action stage, and tell them exactly what you want them to do.** Not that everybody is going to do it, but you can't leave anything out; you can't leave any questions in their minds.

Whenever I start thinking about this whole idea of luring people in rather than shouting at them, the one analogy that always comes to mind is the world of dating, the ritual of romance between a man and a woman. A suitable match doesn't come on too strong; they're more subtle than that. They lure you in. They get you to do the chasing; rather than them chasing you, you're the one chasing them. **And all of it *is* subtle.** It's a ritual. Now, I don't want to complicate things too much, but here's how this would tie into selling: people don't want to be sold, but they do want to buy. So it's all about presentation. In the world of romance, a good match will present himself or herself well.

They'll make efforts to be attractive. They'll do things to get your attention and get you interested, and then inflame your desire. And then they'll present a call to action, which ideally ends up with you getting together with that person and moving the relationship forward.

Your sales letter, and everything you do to maintain contact with your prospects and customers via direct response marketing, is all about presenting yourself well, giving them something attractive to consider. **This is a one-on-one relationship with benefits for both of you.** You're not just trying to get something from them; you're trying to give them something they want very much. Many people new to the game of marketing just don't understand that. The truth is, it's a game of being altruistic in your approach—or at least, fostering the perception of altruism. It's about you making them an offer for something they want—while also showing them what's in it for you. **You're answering all their skepticism.** But it's a very subtle kind of thing, where you want people to perceive that they're the ones chasing you, rather than being chased themselves. That's the way it has to work in the world of direct response marketing. **That's one of the reasons why we use Two Step Marketing. Talking about luring people in rather than shouting!**

Not only that, but **you don't want to tell people too much too fast.** You don't want to throw everything out there at once. You want to hold things back. **This creates that feeling of anticipation that the customers crave:** that there's something more out there, and you're letting them discover things on their own. **It allows them to feel empowered.** People don't want to be sold anything, but they *do* want to buy things, thank goodness. **Memorize that fact: people love to buy things, they just hate to be sold.**

Somebody who's shouting is trying too hard to sell something to somebody. **Somebody who's doing it in a quieter, more subtle way, someone who's soft-selling the product or service, is creating a lure.** That lure is what pulls the customers in and makes them feel empowered—as if they're the ones seeking you out, rather than the other way around. **In their eyes, you aren't selling things to them; they're choosing to buy from you.** Again, all this is very subtle. But you've got to open your eyes to it; you have to get on the other side of the cash register, and really start thinking like a marketer rather than a consumer. Start looking at the relationships you have with companies you buy from over and over again. **Try to determine what it is they're doing that makes you want to do more business with them.**

I recently got a great gift from this company I used to do business with. I let my membership lapse, and the company wants me back. They want to keep getting my money, right? So the owner of the company sent me a really great gift: a book that I fell in love with. Since then, I've told a couple of my friends about it. They went and bought it. It was a great gift that just came out of nowhere! It had no real relationship to what the company was selling, but it just blew me away. I'm going to send a letter to the president of the company thanking him for the gift, and I'm going to start doing business with them again. **All because they did something that just blew me away.**

So look at your own life. **Look at what other people are**

doing to you, or what they're trying to do to you, that causes you to want to seek out these companies and continue to do business with them repeatedly. This isn't happening by accident. They're doing these things in a calculated way; and that can be hard to describe, which is why you've got to experience it, and why you've got to break from the emotional connections that blind you to what those companies are doing. **That's what we call getting on the other side of the cash register.**

Previously, I discussed the two different sales pieces that we're working on right now. One is in development; the other is in testing. The one we're testing is a dollar bill sales letter. The front page of the letter has a brand new, crisp one dollar bill attached to it with what we call "booger glue." And then the letter opens up and says something like, "As you can see, I've attached a crisp one dollar bill to this letter. Why have I done so? Because I want your attention, and I know that the best way to get it is with money. **Since this letter has to do with making money, I thought this would be an appropriate attention-grabber."**

The package comes in a security bag, too, so we spent five times more money on this envelope than the cheapest envelope we could have bought. Then we actually put a dollar bill in the package. **Why? We're trying to make an impression.** We're separating ourselves from everybody else. We're causing them to stand up and take notice. Of course, we're testing this against a mailing *without* the dollar bill, to see whether that dollar is money well spent. In the past, we've tried sending people letters containing honest-to-goodness two-dollar bills. We're going to test that next, if the first test works.

Here again, we're doing things to separate ourselves from others, to get them to take notice, to get people to chase us rather than being chased, to create that lure that we want. **We're not necessarily shouting at people. We're doing something that just blows their minds and separates us from everybody else.**

The second piece is in development as I write this. It won't even be ready for another week. It's a type of sales letter that I've spent dozens of hours working on... but it doesn't look like a sales letter. **It looks like a book, and not even like a regular book, really. It looks totally different.** It's designed to do an effective job of selling by following those four steps of the A.I.D.A. formula, the Attention, Interest, Desire, and Action steps. And yet it does so in a very subtle way, because of the particular service that it sells. We wanted to be much more subtle than normal about it, in fact; we wanted to present ourselves a little bit differently. **It's all about getting attention, you see.** That's why we're creating such a different sales letter, this little booklet that I'm telling you about; and that's why we are mailing dollar-bill letters. That's also why two-dollar bill letters will be our next test. At one point, we even mailed a ten-dollar bill letter. That didn't work, by the way; but we tried it just to see if it would.

That kind of thing is necessary. **As an entrepreneur, as a marketer, you're *always* looking for a way to separate yourself from everybody else.** That doesn't just mean the way something looks and feels; it also means the exact marketing strategies you use. So do think very carefully about what I've just described. It's difficult to put some of this into words, because **we're talking about things that are emotional in nature, where you're trying to be somewhat manipulative in**

trying to making people feel that they're the ones who are coming after you, rather than you coming after them. You're trying to do things that make them feel empowered, instead of being disempowered, as you are whenever somebody's chasing after you, trying to get you to do something you don't want to. People hate that, but they love it when it's their idea. They love it when *they're* the ones doing the choosing and the chasing. The minute they perceive that it's the other way around, that's when they grab their purse or wallet and start backing toward the door.

Now that I've put that out there, let's switch gears a little. As I was contemplating this subject earlier, I started thinking about the qualities of a good leader. That leader could be a sports coach or the leader of a country. You know, a person can be a dictator and still be well liked; or they can be a tyrant, and people can hate them. A good leader, whether in political or sports or elsewhere, demands respect and attention... but not because they're threatening to kill you or cut off your arm. **They do it with the tone of their voice and out of a sincere desire to do what's best for their people.** Those are two different approaches to getting the same results.

So a good leader will garner respect among the people they're leading, but it's not out of a place where they're demanding respect or out of a sense of where the people they're leading are forced to go. Even Communist countries usually have elections, although the elections are rigged. You can make people do what you want them to do; **or, you can lead in such a way that people really want to follow you, even though they aren't required to do so.** There's just something about you that makes them want to pay attention. They like what you say. They feel an affinity for you or towards you. You demand respect not because you're a threat, but because of the way you carry yourself.

As I was thinking about the secrets of a good direct mail letter, I was struck by how much this concept of non-coercive leadership applies here, too. A good direct response campaign doesn't shout at people; it lures them in. What does it mean to shout at people? What does it mean to lure them in? Well, let's go back to the dictator analogy. You can probably force people to buy your product; it wouldn't be legal, but you could hold a gun to someone's head and say, "Give me your money, and I'm going to give you something in return."

Or you can do like the government does, and coerce people by the threat of punishment under our penal system. Supposedly, our tax system is voluntary; but I'm pretty sure that if you don't pay your taxes, they'll come calling and coerce you into paying under threat of penalty and jail time. So our volunteer tax system results in a lot of people paying their taxes, even begrudgingly. Or, you could feel really *good* about the way your government is doing things, and you could feel the tax rates are just and fair, and you're paying them out of a sense of obligation to the betterment of society. **Both attitudes result in tax revenues coming into the government, but one is done under the threat of punishment, while one isn't.**

A good direct mail letter gets the results that you really want, not *just* results—because you *could* coerce people into buying, even without holding a gun to their head. But those methods would be less effective than luring them in, which is why you shouldn't shout or come across as domineering or coercive. **You don't want to make your campaign feel**

desperate, like you have to get their business at all costs. Instead, you want to make them feel like you're presenting an option to them, and ultimately make them feel like they're the ones choosing to do business with you.

When people feel they're being coerced or prodded or pushed into a decision, they become hesitant, reluctant; they pull back or withdraw. You'll lose a lot of transactions that would otherwise happen if people feel like they're being forced or rushed into making a decision they don't necessarily feel comfortable making, where they don't have the time or freedom to choose wisely. On the other side of that coin, if people feel like they want something, that you're making it available to them but you are not coercing them into buying, they'll respond more positively. **If you're just pointing out a need they may have or a solution to one of their problems, then they're in the position of feeling like they're making the decision to do business with you—not that you're forcing them into that decision.**

One of the formulas that we often talk about here at M.O.R.E., Inc. is called the PAS formula: **Problem, Agitate, Solution. That's is a good example of how best to follow this principle, and you see it used all the time in marketing efforts.** Basically, throughout your sales copy, you're pointing out a problem that someone has. You're reminding them of the pain that they're suffering, whether that's physical, emotional, or psychological. You present precisely the range of symptoms they're experiencing, and you start pointing out just how bad it really is. You're agitating the problem—because the funny thing about pain and the human mind is that we tend to become tolerant of the pain we live with on a daily basis. You could have someone in an excruciating amount of physical pain, and over many years of living with that pain, they become tolerant of it. It's not that the pain goes away; they've just adapted their life in such a way as to get by and do the things they need to do just to function. They may not even really be actively thinking about the pain they're in.

But through the agitation phase of the selling process, you remind them of their pain and the symptoms they're suffering through, asking them to think about and remember the days *before* **they had to deal with pain.** Remember taking walks on the beach, or down the street? Remember what it was like to be able to pick up a basketball and play a game before you had knee pain that forced you to the sidelines? You're reminding them of these things because they may have forgotten. At some point, the pain may have become something they live with, without actively thinking about it. **And then, finally, you come along and offer the solution.** The solution, of course, is your miracle formula that some doctor in the jungle recently discovered. You rub a little on the painful area, and within a few seconds the pain starts melting away. Now you've got all the freedom you didn't have before, when you were suffering. If a cure like that was possible, you'd be willing to pay just about anything for it, wouldn't you?

So you've pointed out the problem, you've agitated it and reminded them how real the problem is—and then you've offered your solution. **Well, you're not forcing them to buy that solution.** If they'd like to live with the pain, if they'd like to keep taking 8-10 ibuprofens a day and only experience mild relief, then they're welcome to do that. However, you do have a solution that you're making available. You're pointing out the problem, agitating it, then offering them a solution and letting them decide whether they want to take part in it or not. **You're putting *them* in control.** They're the one deciding whether or not to do business with you.

Look, a good direct mail letter doesn't *have* to scream at people. It doesn't have to be overbearing. **It can just present its case through the sales copy, through the telling of the story and the agitation of the problem, culminating with the solution.** The selling happens through the compelling story you develop, the writing you've done. **A good copywriter doesn't have to force people into buying.** They can tell the story, present the problem and the solution, and through that method create the demand for the product or service being offered. This is one of the reasons why, before you try to sell, you thoroughly need to know who you're selling to. If you've targeted the right marketplace properly, then you're going to be able to make sales without having to shout at people.

Now, I want to make sure that you understand what I mean. I'm not talking about being a weak-minded marketer here. There's a risk when you hear, "Don't shout at people; instead, lure them in." Some people think, "Don't shout? That means I need to be less aggressive." Hah! If you have been around us very long here at M.O.R.E., Inc., then you must know otherwise! **I've written several books on ruthless marketing, and one of the strategies of ruthless marketing is aggressive, no-holds-barred salesmanship.** You have to go after the sale, even if you don't shout. So I'm not talking about weak-minded or unaggressive forms of marketing at all. **I just mean that you should avoid the kind of shouting at people that turns them off** —the kind of overbearing marketing approach that makes them feel you're chasing them too hard, trying to twist their arm to get them to buy. If you're reaching the right marketplace and you're a good copywriter, you don't need to stoop to arm-twisting. They'll do the arm-twisting at their end.

Here's what I mean: if you've done a good enough job writing your sales copy, they'll feel that internal struggle in their own mind as they wrestle with the decision to buy. **Then it'll be them internalizing that decision, not feeling pressure from you.** They'll decide themselves whether what you offer is worth it or not, whether the offer is strong enough for them to say yes to.

Your goal is to do a compelling job of getting them to see what it is you want them to see, in regard to the benefits they'll receive from using your solution. But in the end, it's up to them. Always. You're offering the solution; it's up to them to decide whether to take it or not. Think of a fishing lure: you can't force a fish to bite the lure. **All you can do is present it.** A fisherman might cast his lure out by a tree or a submerged log where the fish-finder picked up the fish, but there's no way to be sure the fish will ever respond, even if there's a big bass hanging out right there. You can toss that lure, sure, and a good fisherman will fish that area for several minutes at least, sometimes longer.

The fisherman might try various ways of presenting the lure; and maybe he'll switch lures and will keep casting to that area, hoping that one of the fish notices the bait. **You present the lure over and over again, several times at least, maybe using several different approaches.** Sometimes you're slowly cranking it. Other times, you're reeling it fast. You're doing different things to try to attract that fish... but ultimately you can't *make* them bite. **They have to decide they want that lure; they have to make the decision on their own.**

It's the same thing with any prospect in your marketplace. You can present the offer to them in a compelling fashion, but ultimately it's up to them to decide whether they want to bite on your offer. You can't make them want to take advantage of what you are selling them, but you *can* help tilt their interest in that direction. So do use aggressive marketing strategies, but don't shout at them. **Present your case as aggressively as you want, then make a compelling argument as to why they need to do business with you, and let them come to you.** Let *them* be the ones feeling like they're doing the chasing. Let them make that decision to buy from you.

Don't ever make your prospects feel you're coercing them, or else you'll end up with bad customers who present you with all kinds of problems, and your refund rates will be high. You'll end up with customers who won't be loyal to you because they liked your products or service; no, they feel like they had to buy, that somehow they were forced into it. Those people are never going to be good customers. They're never going to feel that you provide value to them. They will, instead, feel that they made a bad buying decision, because they were bullied into buying.

Again, the secret of a good direct mail letter is *not* shouting at people: it's luring them in. **You're better off being quietly attractive.** Nobody is attracted to desperation—and if someone wants something from you badly enough to shout, then they're desperate. That's something that people run from, not run towards; what you want is the complete opposite. **So it's a game at some level: however much you want to shout, however much you need their business, you have to be coy and lure them in instead.**

I'm talking about matters of emotion, matters of the heart. So pay close attention to the marketing methods that other people are using, where they're using subtle methods to draw you to them—rather than more aggressive things that turn you away.

CHAPTER FIVE

Working without a strong model is like...
taking a trip without a map.

Drawing Your Map

Working without a strong model is like taking a long trip without a map, which is something that most people would never thinking of doing. If you really think about it, going mapless sounds adventurous and all, and I'm sure there are people who do it. **But a map helps you stay on track.** It gives you information that can save your life, that can save you time, that can save you money. It just makes things more clear.

You wouldn't take a long trip without looking at a map, without studying it, without keeping it close to you, would you?

When it comes to developing marketing materials and ideas, having a good model is like a roadmap. It keeps you on track, it provides needed information, it saves you time, it saves you money—and it makes you *more* money. In this chapter, I'll provide some specific examples of how a good model can do all these things... but first, let me just tell you why a lot of people just don't bother with one.

Most people don't use models as they should because they're stubborn, or they want to be pioneers. They want to believe that their ideas are the best ideas possible, and I understand that. I've been guilty of that my entire life—thinking that I know better, and wanting to do things my own way. Every entrepreneur is motivated by the desire to do things their own way, and frankly, that's one of the best things about being an entrepreneur. **But every strength also has a corresponding weakness, so that's also the worst things about being an entrepreneur:** thinking that you know best, thinking that your way is supreme. **In the end, you may fail to look around and think things through**—to see how other people are doing things, and study the market and get ideas from it. That can be painful at best and, worse, it can be fatal.

When we talk about models, that's what we're really talking about: getting ideas from the marketplace. **I urge you to look at ideas that other people are using; study their material closely.** I've discussed this concept repeatedly throughout this book, as I do in just about every book I write. Again, one of the reasons why people *don't* do it is they just want to be the pioneer; they want to blaze new trails. There's a certain romantic bravado to that concept, and yes, that's an important part of being an entrepreneur. It's an important part of the whole innovation process, admittedly, **but you do also have to pay very close attention to what others are doing. When you do, you'll get all kinds of answers that you wouldn't get if you were trying to do everything on your own.**

You can't create in a vacuum. You just can't. **You have to subject yourself to as many different ideas as you possibly can.** In fact, that's the essence of what creativity is: combining as many different ideas as you can in a variety of combinations, so that you can best appeal to the market you're going after. **Acquiring all those ideas forces you to look outside yourself, to see what other people are doing, to study their work.** You can still think that you're smarter and better than them, and you can still have the cocky attitude you want; but it's a fact that, the most innovative, creative people are the ones who subject themselves to as many ideas as possible. Those who are least creative and least innovative are isolated, doing everything the same way over and over. They never try to reach or expand, because they're not looking outside themselves for new ideas.

So part of the stretching that you do, the growth that you go through, involves studying what other people in your field are doing. And not just what they're doing right, but what they're doing wrong, too. **Many times what they're doing wrong can be just as instructive as what they're doing right.** Once you identify where they're screwing up, you can implement the right processes, correcting the mistakes they're making and profiting along the way. It's all a process of learning.

Look: all the answers you're searching for to help you make money are out there right now. Those answers are in the sales materials and the marketing campaigns your competitors are using. **The real trick is in trying to find the very best things,** to separate the wheat from the chaff if you will, **and then trying to combine them in completely new ways; and that's where true profit lies.** So you're foolish if you're not studying what other people are doing. **You have to subject yourself to as much material as you can.** You must become and remain a student of the entire field. Stay open. Be hungry. **The more you look at what other people are doing, the more common denominators you'll see; all that's part of the process of understanding the market you're in.** Try to be innovative, of course, but not too innovative—because being too innovative can be painful. You know what they say about pioneers: they often get scalped.

Case in point: we're currently involved in a joint venture relationship with Russ von Hoelscher, who has a promotion that's going like gangbusters for him. He's been working it for about six years. **We initially tried to do something similar, but we departed a bit too far from his course... and what we came up with just didn't work, because we were *too* innovative.** We threw in too many of our own ideas, because of course we didn't want to directly copy what he was doing. I'm not talking about stealing here, you see. I'm not talking about plagiarism when I talk about models. **What I mean is that you can take a little of this and a little of that from difference sources, idea-wise, and blend them all together in a unique way.** That's safe and legal, because you can't copyright ideas.

But, well, that process didn't work with this one idea that's making Russ so much money. Finally we gave up, and now we're paying him a small royalty and getting all of his best ideas to work with. **We're not trying to be too innovative anymore.** This new money-making concept didn't really work for us when we tested something like it—but now Russ is helping us every step of the way. **He's giving us the best of the best of his six years in this one money-making project, so in this case, the map is completely clear.**

From here on in, we'll be mirroring the exact same thing that he's doing, so we stand a good chance of increasing our odds of making the most money in the fastest possible time. **And isn't that really what it's all about? Making the most money as easily as you can, as fast as you can, and doing it in the most ethical and honest way? Your models teach you how to do that.** The closer you can get to the model, the better. In this case, we're just adapting everything that Russ is doing. Now that we're licensed, we're going to incorporate every last thing he's doing into our model. That's acceptable, because we have his blessings now. **With this clear new roadmap, it's very likely that this project is going to be successful for us for years, just as it has been for him.**

Here's another example. Back in 1993, our business was struggling. We were just coming off the initial four-year promotion that built the company; but now, all of a sudden, that promotion had quit working. Things were really slow, and I was looking for something to move us forward. Well, one day a sales letter came in the mail from a company that I did business with. It was from the late, great Gary Halbert. Gary's project had to do with making money with computer bulletin boards, a concept that was brand new then. **Most people had never heard of computer bulletin boards, and you may not be very familiar with them now; but basically, they were the precursors to the Internet.**

Gary's sales letter got me so excited, so fired up, that I just *knew* that this was something that could make us a lot of money. But I didn't want to copy Gary; I definitely didn't want to plagiarize. So I spent three months reworking Gary's letter, putting as many of my ideas into it while sticking with his original formula. The way he presented this offer, the structure, the way he set the whole thing up—it was just brilliant. **It took me three months to rewrite the letter because I didn't want to copy Gary; that would have been dishonest.** But I used Gary's letter as a model, and I put my own letter out to the market—**and we made a couple of million dollars very quickly.**

But computer bulletin boards were kind of a fad. **After**

they went away, we revamped that sales letter that took me three months to rewrite and applied it to the Internet... And again, millions of dollars came pouring in.

It all happened because I kept my eyes wide open. I was looking. I was in a desperate situation. I needed something. And then Gary's letter came to me, and it was so absolutely brilliant that it became the model that we used to go on to make millions. **Since then, we've found many other ways to incorporate that selling formula into other offers.** So now, we're kind of copying from ourselves... which I'll talk a little bit about later on. The point is, you have to keep your eyes open, to be absolutely receptive to what's out there. **The Internet is an amazing place to look for ideas, given all of these amazing websites out there selling all kinds of great things.** You can take ideas from all kinds of sources. Also, get on some mailing lists, maintain collections of swipe files, and just spend time looking at, and really studying, what other people are doing.

The more ideas you subject yourself to, the better. You're not just trying to steal. Regarding Gary's idea: I rewrote that sales letter very carefully, spending several months doing that, because I didn't want to steal from Gary. I wanted all my own ideas to be incorporated into it. I wanted it to be written in a careful manner, so that while somebody could see that my letter was similar to his if they had the two side-by-side, even my biggest critics would realize that I hadn't stolen from him. But you know, in a way, I did. You can't copyright an idea, and he had some brilliant ideas. **You've got to recognize brilliance.** The more ideas you look at, the more you'll see the brilliance that's out there. **If you don't look at enough of the ideas that**

other people are doing, you might not recognize that brilliance quite as easily.

So just remember: all the ideas you're looking for are out there right now, and you've got to subject yourself to a lot of material to find them.

I have a place on my property where I do a lot of my creative work. It's a 15,000-square-foot building, and I have things plastered all over the walls. I've saved my best sales material elsewhere too, but **I've got all the really good ideas, the ones that I want to keep thinking about, on those walls.** There's an old saying that goes, "Out of sight, out of mind," and I try to remind myself of that. So I've got all this sales material plastered all over my walls, and as I'm walking around the building, I'm looking at it all. I'm subjecting myself to it. I'm trying to keep it all in mind, trying to pieces these concepts together in new ways. **Again, that's the essence of creativity: combining things in new ways.** So I'm subjecting myself to a lot of different ideas here.

And here's another point that I'd like to make: **after you've been doing this for a while, after you've created enough of your own stuff, you can steal from yourself.** That's how we came up with our initial Internet offers: we took the "How to Make Money with Computer Bulletin Boards" letter that we modeled after Gary Halbert's and incorporated those ideas into our Internet offers when we started marketing websites. That made us millions of dollars more. This is one of the benefits you get if you just stay in the game and stay in the same market long enough. Now, it's also important to look outside your market for other ideas, because part of the essence of creativity is to cast a wide net and incorporate ideas that other people are using that have nothing to do with what you're selling. **So do look for outside concepts to cross-fertilize your thinking, but know that eventually, you'll be able to use your old material as models for new material.**

Recently, I rewrote an old sales letter—and it took me probably an hour total. Basically, all I had to do was make some simple changes to a promotion that worked well for us a few years ago, and I'd created something entirely new out of something that took us dozens of hours to create a few years ago. **So this is a real labor-saving technique. It can help you make a lot more money faster, helping you avoid pitfalls.** It can show you the way, just like a good roadmap will when you're on a journey.

Now, let's go back and take a closer look at something I mentioned earlier: swipe files. **You need to have a file of some sort, or a box, where you keep the best sales material that you've seen other people use, so you can use it as a basis for your models.** I actually have something more like a swipe barn. As I've mentioned, I've got everything laid out so I can just walk through that building and see all of the history there. I can easily find promotions we did ten or fifteen years ago, in some cases, along with a lot of work from other people. Just being able to refer to that, and pore over that material for ideas, is a valuable resource. **You see, it's necessary to have some sort of compass to show you where to go, sometimes: a well-defined direction, rather than trying to venture out and start something from scratch.** This is an important strategy to remember.

When you're writing a sales copy, one of the worst things

you can do is stare at a blank screen. The same thing is true for any writer. The hardest thing is often that first step of getting something down; once you get past that, it's a lot easier to get going. **It's easier to use your models as your springboard, as the starting-off point.** As I said before, you can't patent or copyright an idea... even though people try to do it all the time. **You can't plagiarize an idea either.** Think about the cell phone industry, or the latest computer gizmos and gadgets. Whenever someone comes out with the latest widget, it doesn't take long before everyone else has one that does similar things: the touchscreen mobile phone, for example. Once the first touchscreen mobile came out, everybody soon had one.

Recently, we saw this with the transition from tube-style televisions to flat screens. Once someone cracked the flat-screen code, all of sudden everybody came out with flat-screen TVs — and there were all different kinds. Chris Lakey's first flat was called the D.L.P., which stands for Digital Light Processing — and despite the fact that he bought it just a few years ago, they don't really make many of those anymore. It's an outdated technology for the most part. LCD became the standard that was widely available, and then LED came out as a new technology, and everybody all of a sudden was switching to LED panels for their flat screen TVs. And there was plasma for a while. **This happens all the time: someone innovates, and everybody else copies.** The problem for the innovator is that they're the pioneer, and you know what happens to the pioneer. They end up creating a marketplace from scratch, or they end up going out of the business because they were ahead of their time, or for whatever reason their business just doesn't work out. Other people come in at that point, though, because now there's a built-in marketplace, and their model works, and it's becomes the successful model for everybody else.

That's how it works in the electronics business; your best model will vary according to your marketplace and industry. And it doesn't really matter what you're selling, you're probably not the first one. You're probably not inventing something new, where you've got to create a desire or a demand for the product or service from scratch. There are probably other companies out there that have done what you're trying to do or that are currently selling similar items. You should be on their mailing lists. You should be visiting their websites on a regular basis, collecting swap file material. **Look at their models. What are they using as the hook in their offer? What are they doing to get people to want to respond when selling a similar product to the same marketplace?**

Highlight their sales copy, their literature, their brochures, their fliers, their sales letters, their website. Print it all out. Figure out what they're doing to get their message across. Look for the most successful models — not the companies that are failing, or that you think will fail. **Then take what they're doing, and do it in a slightly different way. Use your own USP, of course: you've got your own unique story or approach that makes you different from everybody else in your marketplace.** But you're using their basic ideas to sell similar products to the same marketplace.

As I said in the introduction to this chapter, **working without a strong model really is like taking a trip without a map.** It's deciding that you're just going to wander aimlessly through the countryside; you're not really sure where you're going, and you've got no real time-frame for getting there. Which roads you end up on don't really matter. It doesn't matter how many highways or side streets you travel; you're just out driving around, and eventually you'll get somewhere and you'll stop.

But that's not the way most people travel! Most people plan everything out in advance, and study all the maps beforehand. Chris Lakey goes so far as to print out directions online, looking at all the possible alternate routes that he could take on the trip. He's very detail-oriented when it comes to planning out a trip and where he's going to be driving, how he's going to get there, and exactly what's going to happen along the way. That's the way most people are—maybe not to the degree Chris is, but to the extent that they want to know where they're going, and they want to know what roads they're taking to get there. They want to know how long it's going to take, and they want all that figured out before they start.

And so if you're in business and you're just floating by, haphazardly advertising and not paying any attention to your results, then you're driving without a map. You're not really focusing on the route you're taking to success. At best, you're just getting by, not analyzing the results of your actions much. Maybe you do a little bit of advertising and see some results, so you do a little bit more. Pretty soon years go by, and maybe your business fails. Or maybe you're struggling to survive—making a little profit, but not doing well in general. **The flip side of that is working with strong models, which gets you where you want to go. You've got a roadmap. Your path to success is already paved.** You know exactly what you're trying to accomplish, and you're using strong models to accomplish that and reach your goals.

As each ad campaign comes and goes, you know the results you received. You have it all mapped out. **You know what worked and what didn't.** You move forward with those results, looking for newer, better models that will work better in the future. **You're constantly adapting, sure, but you're on the path to success.**

Recently, there was a TV commercial that showed a guy on a path to retirement. They kept telling him to stay on the path, even though he would look off and there would be a window with a boat in it, or something else that he would to want to buy right now. They would say, "Just stay on the path." The arrow was pointing ahead, not into the window where the boat was. The idea is that if he just stays on the path, he'll reach his goals and he'll retire the way he wants to. If he buys the boat and goes deeper into debt, he's missing the mark, straying off the path.

I think that commercial was a good illustration of this point. **If you don't waver from these strong models, the road maps to success, then they'll help you reach your destination.** That doesn't mean there won't be detours; it doesn't mean you don't occasionally make decisions that don't pay off or that end up hurting more than helping, or things like that. **It just means that your path is all pre-calculated, using strong models to help pave the way and to get you where you're going faster.**

Using a strong model will always help you on your road to success. And remember, just see it as a game. Look at it as an enjoyable search for fulfillment, for success. As the saying goes, half the fun is getting there.

CHAPTER SIX

True power *is* **knowing your strengths and weaknesses.**

Don't lie to yourself about these two areas. Most people tend to overestimate their chances of success and underestimate their chances of failure. You must become stronger in the areas you are already strong in and delegate (not abdicate) your weakest areas.

Finding True Power

True power is knowing both your strengths *and* your weaknesses. Don't ever lie to yourself about these two areas. Most people tend to overestimate their chances of success in the business, because they ignore those things they're weak in. That's a recipe for disaster. **To truly succeed, you need to become stronger in the areas you're already strong in and delegate, not abdicate, your weakest areas.**

Let me start with the difference between delegation and abdication. When you abdicate something, you just turn it over to somebody and say, "Oh, you take care of it for me." But you don't follow up on it; you don't have a hand in any part of the process. When you delegate something, you're still handing it off to somebody else, but you're also taking some personal responsibility in making sure it gets done. You're following up, trying to make a difference. You're trying to contribute what you *can* contribute, and you're making sure it's done correctly.

Entrepreneurs tend to be abdicators rather than delegators. Personally, I'm a firm believer in letting others do what they do, while I do what I do. I'm all about trying to find the very best people possible to do what I'm weak at, and I do my share of abdication. That's another weak area of mine. Maybe, as I get older and move forward, I'll delegate more than I abdicate; but at the moment I do abdicate a lot. **I'm also a big believer in becoming stronger in the areas that I'm already**

good at. It's a lesson that I've had to learn the hard way.

My wife Eileen ran the company for its first 14 years, before she had to step down due to multiple sclerosis. As her disease progressed, her doctors said, "You can't do this anymore. You can't handle the stress." So she stepped down, and I stepped up. You know, I always thought that I could do a better job of running the company than she did, because, well, **she made it look easy.** And she didn't really put in as many hours as *I* was willing to put in. She didn't care as deeply as I do. **To her, it was just a job she did—although she was very, very good at it.** I failed to appreciate that. I failed to recognize her strengths and her talents.

To make a long story short, I tried to take over the day-to-day operations of M.O.R.E., Inc., and after about two and a half years, I waved a white flag. Today, we have a great General Manager named Shelley Webster who runs everything. She does an awesome job, and I'm back to doing what I did for the first 14 years of our company: **I'm focused on the marketing, the things that attract and retain customers, the things that are innovative in nature and keep our company moving forward. It's what I do best.**

So many entrepreneurs make the mistake that I made when my wife stepped down: they try to do it all, including all those things they're no good at. Most entrepreneurs are lousy managers. They can barely manage themselves, let alone anybody else—much less a whole company.

The strengths that make somebody a good entrepreneur are *not* the same strengths, necessarily, required to manage a company. Entrepreneurs are focused on looking forward, staying ahead of the game by creating and developing new things, supplying the vision and working *on* the business, not in it. **Managers are focused on the day-to-day aspects of the business. They're stable people, and have to pay close attention to details.** Quite frankly, a lot of the work they do is way too monotonous for most entrepreneurs. We're addicted to the chase, addicted to the adventure of the company.

Just because you *can* do something, doesn't mean that you *should* do it. During those two and half years that I tried to run everything at M.O.R.E., Inc., I would come home absolutely exhausted, just totally beat up, and I would fall asleep on my favorite chair. My wife would ask me what I did that day, and most days, I couldn't even give her a good answer. I knew that I had worked my ass off, since I was thoroughly exhausted, but what I did was the same as most entrepreneurs do when they're put in that position. I spent all day long putting out brushfires (metaphorically, of course). **I was solving all these little problems that cropped up, depleting all of my energy by trying to do it all.**

I see many entrepreneurs playing that game, and it's a losing game, really—because the strength lies in focusing your energy, rather than scattering it. When I talk about focusing, **I'm talking about focusing on the two areas of the business that actually produce profits, instead of anything that actually costs the company money.** If done right, these things will always be profitable. **The first is marketing,** which is all the things you do to differentiate yourself in the eyes of your prospective buyers, and then to attract and retain the largest group of the very best customers for the longest time possible, for the most profit over the long haul. **The second is**

innovation: all the things you're doing to re-invent yourself, as you continue to develop new products and services based not just on the things that worked in the past, but also on the way your market is changing and evolving. Innovation involves looking for creative solutions that cause more people to buy from you, and either make your competitors tremble with fear or go green with envy. Those are the two things that most entrepreneurs are really good at anyway.

If you're a managerial type, no doubt you love to pay attention to details. You're a stable person who likes to take care of all the daily plotting. If that's the case, then you need to find somebody to partner up with who's more entrepreneurial. Conversely, if you're entrepreneurial, you need to partner up with somebody who's a good manager, or otherwise build a team of other people to support all the areas you're weak in.

That's it in a nutshell. **Do more of what you're already good at. Become stronger in all the areas you're already strong in, then delegate as many of the areas you're weak in as possible to the very best people you can surround yourself with.** That will make you more money. It will give you more pleasure. You'll find yourself enjoying the process a lot more. You'll get more done, and you'll achieve bigger things in the end.

Again, so many entrepreneurs are trying to wear all the hats in their businesses. They're trying to do it all, so they can't focus where they need to. Instead, they end up spending a lot of time doing what I call minimum wage work. If it's not minimum wage work, at least it's the kind of work you could hire somebody else to do better and more cheaply. When you do this, you're wasting money. **So what you need to do is take a really good character inventory.** As someone said thousands of years ago, "Know Thyself." Most people *don't* know themselves as well as they should. They've never really taken a good look at their strengths—and more significantly, they've never gotten honest with themselves about their potential weaknesses.

They're jacks of all trades. Those are average people. They're kind of good at a lot of things, but they're great at nothing. Is that the way you want to be? I don't think so. The people we admire most in this world are those who are true masters at what they do, those who rise above the crowd. **In order to develop those kinds of skills and become a master, you've got to focus tightly on a few things.** You can't just be doing a whole bunch of different things. In business, as long as those few things are related to the areas of marketing and innovation, and as long as you can surround yourself with a good team of people who can fill in all the holes, then you can build something that will truly be revolutionary—and you can achieve all of your dreams.

It sounds simplistic, sure, but within that simple framework, there's a lot of complexity. I don't mean to over-generalize, not at all. Yet what I've just described to you is a true recipe for building a successful company and making millions of dollars, if that's what you want to do. **So sit down and have a good, introspective discussion with yourself. Lay it all out there, strengths and weaknesses alike.** Most of us are unwilling to do that. We tend to focus on our strengths, and would prefer to shove our weaknesses under a metaphorical rug instead of deal with them. **Well, one of the ways to succeed in business is to know the difference between a strength and a weakness. Don't lie to yourself about these two things!** Most people do, so they tend to overestimate their chances of success.

That's especially true of optimists; and honestly, optimism is great, but it doesn't help you (or anybody else) if it's misguided and ignores reality.

If you constantly feel like things are going to go better than they do, or if you're always overestimating your likelihood of success, then you're going to tend to come up short. When you come up short consistently, you're going to ask yourself, *Why does this always happen?* You need look no further than the optimist in you to know why that is. You tend to minimize the risk of failure, or the risk that your success won't be as big or as much as you thought it would be.

So the power comes in knowing which things you excel at and which things you need help with, and focusing on those things that you do well. Delegation is an important part of this; one of the best things you can do for your business is build a team of people who help you excel in the areas you're lacking in. In order to do that, you first have to acknowledge that you can't do it all. So what if you're a good jack-of-all-trades? That just means you don't excel at anything. A lot of people try to wear all the hats in their business; they try to be the salesclerk, the cashier, the stocker, the advertiser, the customer service rep. In between that, they're trying to squeeze in accounting and handling the taxes. If there's an issue or dispute with the IRS, they have to deal with that. They work with the suppliers and venders, too.

So they do it all—and maybe they manage okay, but they wear themselves out, and the truth is that they probably aren't very good at all those things. Maybe they miss out on some tax deductions, but by and large they make sure their taxes are filed on time and they don't get audited that often. They're fine at washing down the windows and dusting the shelves, but that's minimum wage work. Maybe they're really good at marketing, so they manage to bring the customers in, but the accounting side of the business suffers. Or maybe it's the other way around.

So a person trying to wear all those different hats all at the same time *may* get by. They may not have any serious problems because they tend to get it all done... but they don't have anything that they do well at, so their business doesn't do as well as it could. On the other hand, the business owner who recognizes strengths and weaknesses experiences a different life. If they're good at sales, they may play the part of the head salesperson, but they've got a clerk who works behind the counter that they're paying a fair wage to. They've got an accountant who does all the books for them. **The business runs like a well-oiled machine, because they've got players handling the various roles that they're weak at while they focus on doing what they do best.** That's the difference between someone who recognizes their strengths and weaknesses and someone who doesn't. Look: it's better to be good at and get better at something, than to be mediocre in a bunch of different things, and continue to be mediocre. So understand your strengths and weaknesses. Don't lie to yourself about the two. Be honest with yourself.

Recognize what you are good at and what you aren't, and get help: have other people step in and do those things for you that you can't, or that aren't reasonable for you to do at your pay scale. To do otherwise would be like deciding to do all your home maintenance, even when you're not mechanically inclined. **Here's a funny story that happened recently, and it**

MONEY MACHINE

illustrates just how silly it is to think that you can do everything on your own.

Chris Lakey and his family live in a fairly new house, built a little over a year ago; they're the first owners. He says that one of the reasons they opted for a new house was that he and his wife both know that he's not mechanically inclined. So one weekend recently, they discovered this sewage-like smell coming from one of the storage rooms in the basement, where the furnace is. When Chris went down there and smelled that, he asked himself, "What in the world is going on here?" He's no plumber, so he immediately picked up a phone and called one.

The funny part is that the plumber Chris uses actually handles heating and cooling too, and they accidentally sent out the heating and cooling guy, because he said it was in the room where his furnace was. So he's showing the technician what's wrong, and this guy's obviously not a plumber, either. He looks at Chris and says, "OK, well, there's nothing wrong with the furnace. I can't really do anything for you. But I'll go back and send the right guy out." So he goes back and Chris gets a call from a guy who says, "I guess you've got a plumbing issue of some kind, right? I'll be out there in a few minutes."

So he comes out and he goes into the room, and obviously smells that there's something wrong. He goes over to a little drain in the floor close to the sump pump area, where there's a little pipe that comes off the furnace to drain off the condensation from the cooling system in the summer. He gets down on the floor, sticks his nose right up to that pipe, and immediately pops back up and goes "Yep." Then he immediately tells Chris something that he ends up getting charged a full hour for, even though the visit took all of two minutes. Now, Chris will never have this problem again, so he learned a lesson here. This is what the plumber told him: in the summertime, moisture comes out of that pipe and into that hole. That creates sort of a seal, where the water sitting there keeps the smell in the septic system, where it belongs.

Now, this happened in the winter, so there wasn't any moisture coming down from the condensation pipe; that seal had dried up, letting the smell out. That was what caused the problem. So what he told Chris was an essentially free solution that Chris says he should have figured out himself: dump a gallon of water into that hole, and problem solved. Sure enough, it worked; within 24 hours, the smell was gone. Later, Chris got a bill for an hour-long visit that actually took a couple of minutes to handle.

Now, that was an expensive lesson, I suppose. But Chris says that had he tried to figure something out on his own, he might have busted the pipes and tried to go in looking for a solution to a problem that didn't really exist, because the only problem was that water had dried up in that hole. **So the plumber's expertise was valuable, in that he was able to cure something in 60 seconds that Chris probably couldn't have ever figured out on his own.** Obviously, Chris knows where his weaknesses are when it comes to home repairs! He's a great marketer, and if you get him into a political discussion, he can certainly hold his own. But ask him how to fix a plumbing or electrical situation, and he's not your person. **He knows his strengths and his weaknesses—and he knows who to call on to help him with things that he can't do on his own.**

That's how it needs to work in your business, too. It's all about being a better delegator, and knowing when you should do something and when you shouldn't. **Never be afraid to have a team, to build an organization around you!** Maybe your team is composed of employees, or maybe it's composed of consultants: an accountant who doesn't work for you directly, but whom you hire to manage your business's finances or the numbers behind them. You're paying them to provide a service for you. **Whatever it is, you're building a team of people who are there to pick up the slack for those areas you're weak in.** So know your strengths and work in those areas, and then let other people help you in the areas that you're not as strong in.

One of the most important things you can do is be a good marketer for your business. You can delegate a lot of things, but **delegating your marketing is rarely a good idea.** Let everything else be your weakness, because **marketing should be your strength, and** *that's* **where you'll find the most power in determining success or failure of your business.** You can rely on other people to do all the other things that have to be done for your business to succeed. Again, your true power is in knowing your strengths and weaknesses, and then not lying to yourself, and *then* finding other people to delegate to in order to get those things done that still have to be done.

This an excellent way to develop your personal power as a businessperson, because it lets you focus on what you're best at. There are basically two kinds of people, you see: those who get paid for what they know, and those who get paid for what they do. **The first group always makes more money than the second, so master something. Become a master of marketing and innovation.** That's my recommendation to you.

CHAPTER SEVEN

Find good people — and stay loyal to them:

It's always easier to maintain a relationship you already have — than to go out and start a new one.

—⁓—

Find Good People
and Stay Loyal to Them

The basic idea here is simple: it's always easier to maintain a relationship that you already have, rather than to go out and start a new one. **This is as true inside a business as it is in a personal relationship, or in a relationship with one of your clients.**

My favorite metaphor for a company is that it's like a fine old watch, the kind where you open up the back and see all these little mechanisms moving in place. There might be 60 different gears, springs, and cogs in there. **Some are fairly big, some are tiny, but all of them are important—even the smallest gear. If you pull it out, the watch just doesn't work.**

That's the way I see a company. It consists of all of the employees you surround yourself with, your suppliers, your joint venture relationships, your banker, your accountant, your attorney, and more. **It really *is* all about surrounding yourself with the very best people possible.** And what does that mean? **Well, first of all you're looking for the most honest people you can find.** That can be difficult, but basically, you're looking for people you can count on, those with real stability. Flaky people are sometimes very, very talented, but you can't really depend on them, so you can't maintain any kind of a significant relationship with them.

Find people who are talented in an important area; this is

vital. **Find people who are really good at what they do, who have poured their hearts and souls into it, who have paid a price over an extended period of time to develop those skills. Those are the people you need to surround yourself with.** Hopefully they'll be people you can count on, people who like you and whom you like. That helps, but it's not absolutely necessary. You can actually have people on your team that you *don't* like... but usually those are the people that you don't work as closely with.

Finding people who are strong in all the areas you're weak in requires some character inventory both on a plus and minus scale, and then, ideally, **you have to find someone you believe will stay around to grow with you—someone you can see having a long-term relationship with.** As I mentioned a moment ago, the relationship doesn't have to be perfect; it just needs to be workable. Again, some of this does sound like basic common sense, but in a minute I'll tell you why, for a lot of people, it isn't common sense at all. A lot of people are violating this principle for their own reasons.

I feel that when you find those good people, you have to do everything possible just to hold on to them. Now, you can't have full control over someone unless you have a gun to their head, and you don't want to do that! **Instead, you have to do things that make it as advantageous as possible for them to continue to want to work with you.** That's all you can do. First of all, it requires a certain willingness to go through all the ups and downs with them. Nobody is perfect; some people will let you down occasionally. Some people will let you down a lot, but if they're basically good people, then you can stick it out with them. **You go through the thick and the thin and you do things to care for them, and try to maintain a good relationship with them.**

You see, it's all about relationships; in fact, that's what all business is about. A relationship is a two-way street, never a one-way road. **It involves give and take on the parts of all the parties involved, so you have to be responsible for what you *can* be responsible for, and that's giving as much as you can possibly give.** You're there for people. You care about them. You try to do things to encourage them and make life fun for them. So make your business a positive place to work, a place that's exciting and enjoyable. Personally, I look at the people I work with almost as extended family (some more than others, of course). You're with family for the long haul.

Now, again, you may think that all this is common sense. It *sounds* like common sense: **find good people, and stick it out with them for the long haul.** And yet a lot of entrepreneurs are too independent for this. They want to do everything themselves, and they think they can. Some entrepreneurs really are talented, and they *can* do everything themselves; that's part of the problem. They're right and wrong simultaneously.

Remember: just because you *can* do something doesn't mean that you *should*. But still, a lot of entrepreneurs want to wear all the hats. They don't realize the vital necessity of a team. Remember the metaphor of the fine watch, where every gear and cog is important. When you apply this to the business world, every moving part of the watch represents a different person you work with, or at least the relationships that you have with your key people. That's a foreign concept to a lot of these highly driven, very independent entrepreneurs.

In the end, instead of attracting good people, they run them off. They want to control everything and are very difficult to work with. It's something I've struggled with a lot myself. Yet, I will say this about myself: even at the beginning, there was a part of me that instinctively knew that I wasn't going to make it all by myself. I wasn't born with the curse of being so talented that I could do everything on my own. **And I *do* think that being multi-talented can be a curse, because it gets in the way of success.** Multi-talented people can do everything themselves; I can't. Somewhere deep inside, I knew that. Back when I first started getting ambitious, when I first started kindling my desires for making millions of dollars, I realized I was going to need a team if it was going to happen.

I first went into business with my best friend, back in December 1985. Our friendship was destroyed because of it; nine months later we weren't friends anymore. **Yet if it wasn't for Gary, my best friend at the time, I probably wouldn't have had the courage to step out on my own and do it.** Gary was full of courage, and he supplied that necessary fuel that got the rocket off the launching pad. Later, I met my wife, Eileen, and from that point forward everything started working.

By then, I had been committed to being my own boss for several years. Eileen and I developed a solid business partnership. I'd like to say that she's my equal, but the truth is that Eileen is my superior in many ways. She's earned my full respect and she's very talented—and without her, it would have never worked. **She ran our company for first 14 years, and because of her, we survived. She put together an amazing**

98

management crew that survived me running the place after she stepped down as CEO. See, I tend to be just like those entrepreneurs that I talked about. I was difficult to work with when I was younger, extremely abrasive sometimes. I would confront people, I would offend people, I would yell at them. These are qualities I've worked really hard to let go of.

Hey, I was a jerk OK? I was another word that starts with an A—you know the one. **I was highly driven, and I was extremely hard to work with.** So many entrepreneurs are like that. Now, that's not an excuse; there's no excuse for that kind of behavior. You have to learn to transcend that. **But thank goodness I inherited a good staff.** The best thing I've done in the 10 years since is that I haven't run any of them off. The good ones I inherited from Eileen when I took over have continued to work with me. Since then, we've also put a few other key people into place.

These are good, talented people, people that I'm so grateful I work with on a daily basis. Chris Lakey is an excellent example. **He and I are a tag team duo when it comes to developing the products and services that keep our company on the cutting edged.** That's not to say that our other management staff don't play a key role in helping us shape and form those ideas, because they certainly do. But it's as part of a team, and they see the importance of that.

The acronym for "team" that I like the best is "Together Everybody Achieves More." It's the synergistic effort of a good group of people who continue to work together on a regular basis, and the sum is far greater than the individual parts. That's a big part of what synergy is all about. It's almost like working together involves an amplification process. Instead of 10 plus 10 plus 10 equaling 30, 10 times 10 times 10 equals 1,000.

That's the kind of synergistic power I'm talking about. **When you put good, talented people together who have complimentary skills and abilities, they all have a way to contribute, bringing certain qualities to the table that combine to make the team more powerful.** That's what makes small companies succeed, and it also gives you joy in life, too. I feel sorry for these very smart, multitalented entrepreneurs who end up running everybody off, because they have no personal relationships of real value. Sure, they might succeed at some level; but in the end, what makes the game of business worthwhile is the people we surround ourselves with. It's not just people working together in the way that most people think about working. We treat it as a game. **A large part of keeping these good people is to do things that make it fun, so everybody can enjoy coming to work.** It's not the drudgery that some people experience, where they have to pull themselves out of bed and force themselves to do it on a daily basis.

Now, even if you're not running the day-to-day aspects of the business—if, say, your more of a financier than a manager or an entrepreneur—then you still need to have good people in place to keep the company moving forward. **It's especially critical to you have some kind of an Office Manager or a General Manager for your business, someone who can run everything on a day-to-day basis;** and when you find that person, they're probably worth whatever it is they want you to pay them (within reasonable limits, of course). The talent they bring to your business will be very valuable; and if they do their job well, it will be very difficult to replace them, and will come at great cost.

There was a time back in the mid-1990s, when Eileen was running the company, that we had a situation where the Office Manager left. I don't remember what made it happen—I believe they had to move for some reason—but suddenly we didn't have an OM. I do remember that we ended up bringing in someone who wasn't familiar with our business, and wasn't familiar with the way we did things. Now, both Eileen and I have a somewhat loose management style when it comes to the company; by that, I mean, the company isn't run like a tightly-run factory or something where we maintain total control over our employees at all times, and if you happen to catch someone in the hall not walking as fast as they should be, you would fire them. We've never been that way... **but the new OM was pretty militant in the way she ran things. She tried to control the company from the management position, and it was an incongruent fit.** She wasn't here long. I think this principle of staying loyal to people and maintaining a relationship you already have is apropos here. It's much easier than going out and starting a new one.

In this case, the principal applied in more ways than one. Hiring a new Office Manager ended up being a complicated process, because the person we hired had no experience in our industry, and had no idea that our office had been running smoothly before the old manager left. **We were doing okay, by my recollection, and she came in and rocked the boat. Suddenly, things weren't as smooth as they had been.** There was a rough adjustment period that we never could overcome, and she just wasn't here long. Maybe if we'd given it another six months or a year, it might have worked out better; but it takes so long to train a new person on what you expect and how the process works that it's not worth dealing with the issue unless you have to.

That may seem a little mercenary, but it's just good business. If you've got someone you've already trained or who already knows your model, knows your systems, and in general knows how you want to operate, then it's valuable to you to do whatever it takes to keep them. In some cases, that means paying them a high wage, whereas maybe you could get away with paying somebody else a little bit less. **It's better to pay them well so you can you retain them; maybe you give them a nicer office, too. You do things that are favorable to them, because you want to treat them well and make them want to stay.** You don't want to do something that would rock the boat and make them want to leave, or give them a reason why they may not be comfortable where they are.

Keeping good people is an important part of this whole model of keeping your business running as optimally as possible. That's true whether you're talking about an Office Manager, a sales team member, or someone in customer service or any other part of your business. **If you've got good people there, it's much easier to make sure that things are going well with them rather than bring someone else in.** There's a certain cost of doing business, and those costs go up dramatically when you have to train somebody from scratch.

Let's say you need a new salesperson on the floor

immediately, so you run an ad and bring someone in. Well, that doesn't happen as quickly as you might want it to, because the first thing you have to do is teach them your company's policies and show them how your business works in general. Then they have to be trained on your products and services and how to present them to prospective customers. This may take as little as a week if you have a fairly simple business model, but it may take as much as a month if the business model is complicated. **All this time, you're paying them to learn on the job and get enough experience to get out there and be a good salesperson.** You spend a lot of money and go through some headaches, **and of course, there's always the risk that things won't work out and you'll have to start over from square one.**

It's much easier to take someone who's already in the system and make sure that they stay happy and that *you* stay happy with that relationship, so there's no reason for them to want to go anywhere else. Find good people in your company and stay loyal to them. Make them happy and give them a reason to stay, and you'll be much better off and much further ahead than if you're constantly in a state of flux — if you're always bringing in new people or always moving people around, so you lack stability in those important positions within your company.

By the way, this concept doesn't just apply to people working within your company! **Consider suppliers and vendors, for example. It's a lot easier to keep working with those that you've already worked with than it is to find a new one.** Our printer is a good example: we've been working with him since the early 1990s. He's been with us through thick and thin—through the good times, when we're doing really well, and through the not-so-good times when we've struggled a bit. He's been there when promotions have been working really well, and when things don't work, and he's printed all kinds of specialty items for us or had them outsourced. By now, he knows our business very well. He knows what our main goals are. **He's about as close to our company as any supplier has ever been, and he knows the kinds of things we're trying to accomplish with our business, and so it's not uncommon for him to bring us a suggestion.** Not too many suppliers or vendors will, outside of the occasional salesman who's just trying to sell you something; but our printer, Steve, will actually come to us with suggestions on things we might want to try or things we might want to test. **He knows our business, and that allows that relationship to continue to flourish.**

If we were to decide to use a new printer, there would be some growing pains. We would have to submit official requests for bids, we would have to show them what we're doing now, and they could try to see if they could do a good job for us. **I know for a fact that we've achieved a certain status within Steve's company, so we get good prices because of the relationship we have.** Well, if we were just to go find a new printer we would probably get charged their standard rate—the premium rate they charge people who just come in off the street, because we've got no relationship with them... whereas our existing printer will do things special for us at a very reasonable rate.

For example, there are times where if we need something printed quickly, and we need only a few copies, Steve will run them through for free. He'll do that for us because he's getting enough other business that he's happy to throw that in as an extra service. In some past events, we've made up big poster boards to display around the room, and he'll print those for us quickly. **You see, that relationship serves both us and him.** If we were to do business somewhere else, he would have to go find new clients. We represent a certain portion of his business that's fairly consistent and automated. He knows that he's going to have new printing jobs from us on a fairly regular basis, because he knows our business and *knows* that he's our printer. If we were to go somewhere else, he would lose that business and have to go chase it down somewhere else.

So Steve is willing to give us good deals, willing to do the kinds of things that keep us happy as clients. The relationship is mutually beneficial; it serves us both to keep that relationship strong and to otherwise maintain it so that everybody's happy. And he's just one supplier. We have a lot of suppliers who are that way, though Steve is probably our biggest supplier in that respect, and the one that it's most important to have that kind of relationship with. Now, we use the post office a lot too, but I wouldn't say we have a great relationship with them. I don't know that anybody does, but still, they've certainly done some things to help us out. **In fact, we have a mail truck that comes and picks up our mail daily to take it on to the bigger processing center in Wichita.** So, we have some similar relationships that are established, but Steve is probably the best example of why it's important to cultivate your vendor relationships, to make sure that no one becomes unhappy—because maintaining those relationships really does help both sides.

Loyalty to your customers is also important; that is, finding good people and staying loyal to them also applies to customer relationships. **You'll find that your biggest profits come from your best customers, and it's much easier and more profitable to sell to existing customers than to go out and get new ones.** Existing customers know you, like you, and trust you; there's already a built-in, established relationship. **When you go to a new customer and try to get them to decide to do business with you, there's is a built-in *resistance*.** They don't know you, so they're afraid of being taken advantage of somehow, or they're afraid of not getting a good deal, or they're afraid of paying too much—they're afraid of all kinds of things that make them fearful of saying yes and doing business with you, whereas with an existing customer those walls are already torn down. **The resistance is already gone because there's an established relationship.**

It's much easier and more profitable to do business with someone who's already done business with you than to do business with a new customer for the first time, and that means your customers can become loyal to you and you loyal to them. **You want to take care of them, because they're the lifeblood of your business.** Sure, new customers are required to keep your business going and keep profits flowing through your business, but you make most of your profits serving your existing customers.

Let's say you've got a booming business, and you bring in 1,000 new customers every single week—and you never do anything to build relationships with them. You have a customer turnover of 100%. You bring people in, you do business with them once, and then they never have any reason to do business with you again. **But if you build relationships with those 1,000 people, then by Week Two, you've got not just 1,000 new customers, but also 1,000 *existing* customers. In Week Three, you've got 2,000 existing customers and 1,000 new ones again, and it just keeps snowballing, building a customer base of people who already have a relationship with you.** These are people who are more likely to trust you and do more and more business with you.

So being loyal to them means continuing to think of them, continuing to offer them additional services and products related to what they already bought from you once. You know they're interested in certain kinds of products and services because you've already sold them some of those, so you come back to them on a regular basis to offer additional products and services like those they already bought. You give them more incentive to do more business with you, by making them special offers as a preferred customer and in general by doing things to keep them coming into your business over and over again. **The relationship is mutually beneficial.**

You need to do that consistently, working to build loyal customers by being loyal to them; and they will, in turn, be loyal to you, and can provide you with a lifelong steady income. You'll have them doing more business with you, more frequently, especially if your business involves some kind of consumable or some other mechanism where they have to come back on a regular basis. Even if it doesn't, as long as you continue to offer high-quality products or services similar to what they already bought, they'll be inclined to do more business with you. **Continue to provide value and continue to make them special offers that make them feel welcomed and encouraged to do business with you.** Do that, and they *will* be there to provide you with ongoing sales and profits.

So being loyal to your customers, and having them in turn be loyal to you, is another strategy in this formula for maintaining relationships that you already have, rather than constantly going out and starting new ones. **Being loyal to employees, vendors, and customers really can provide you with a business that will be profitable for the years to come.** My company is proof of that. That's how we work. If you'll do the same, if you'll be loyal to those three groups of people, they will be loyal back; and as a result, you can build a thriving business that provides you with profits right now and well into the future.

Let's go back to my watch analogy. **A profitable business is like a well-oiled machine, all the parts of which mesh and work together to produce success.** All these people have their own agendas, not just by category but individually. You really can't force anybody to do anything, so you have to persuade them to do so by making things as advantageous for them as possible, so they'll be attracted to you and want to stay with you. **But so many entrepreneurs are penny-wise and dollar foolish!** They never build relationships with their suppliers, or consultants or freelancers, or any of the professionals who can help support their business, because they're always trying to get the best prices on everything. That's all they care about. They're not in it long-term with anybody.

Even when it comes to employees and building a

management team, once again they're selfish and greedy; they're driven to succeed at any cost, and they lack the people skills they need. **So they run off everybody who's really talented.** I've seen this; in fact, I know somebody who suffers from this problem right now. They can't stand having anybody better than they are working side-by-side with them. It threatens them. So whenever somebody comes along that they perceive is better than them, they run them off. I'm not sure they're even aware that they're doing that, but it's happening.

And look, sometimes you've got to pay more for quality. When it comes to people, remember this: **good people don't cost you money, they *make* you money.** I'm not just talking about consultants and freelancers or similar professionals, **I'm talking about your staff, the people that you work with daily.** Some entrepreneurs and small business people see all of this as nothing but a cost to them. But if they were *really* to focus on this word "relationship," really study it and think it through, I think it would eventually sink into their heads—even for some of these very greedy, self-centered, totally driven entrepreneurs who are mildly sociopathic. It may take them years to just think about the word "relationship," and all it implies, but they can get there. It's a give-and-take, you see; it's a two-way street. **It means that you have to be there for other people if you want them to be there for you.**

All that just sounds so much like common sense... but if you keep your eyes wide open, you'll see that plenty of people are out there violating this common-sense strategy every day of every week. When it comes to the customer aspect of it, they're chasing new customers constantly, instead of trying to do more business with their existing customers. When it comes to employees, they just look at the cost of everything, and end up hiring people who are cheaper, maybe, but who also lack the talents and abilities to contribute to their companies and to provide those synergistic qualities I talked about earlier. When it comes to suppliers, they're out there looking for the lowest-priced dealers, and often those people are fly-by-night operators who won't be around long-term anyway.

So think it through. Don't just minimize what I'm talking about here because it *does* sound simple. That's the good news. Sometimes people want things to be complicated, so anything that sounds too simple just rolls right off of them. **Yet what I'm describing here doesn't have to be hard.** If you're looking for a good book that perfectly illustrates every single thing that I've just talked about in this way, one about a company that started with almost no money and is now a household word throughout the world, just pick up a copy of *Behind the Golden Arches*. Now, it's an old book, written in the mid-1980s, so it's terribly out of date. Yet if you were to just read that book cover-to-cover a few times, I think you would really, truly understand the value of what I've just talked about, and how it could be worth billions in profits.

Of course, the book is about the McDonald's Corporation out of Des Plaines, Illinois, a company that everybody in the whole world knows about. **McDonald's is all about relationships, in every way, shape, and form.** Why that book isn't required reading in every college business course is beyond my comprehension.

CHAPTER EIGHT

The insiders are usually blind. Only an outsider can objectively look at something in a fresh, new way.

The Insiders Are
Usually Blind

You know, it often takes an outsider to look at something in a fresh, innovative way. This is especially true in business. **Small business people in particular tend to be blind to new ideas.** They fall prey to so-called "marketing incest," where everybody's just following the next person—and so the blind are leading the blind. **Ultimately, they're all doing exactly the same thing that their competitors are doing.** There's nothing exciting, unusual, or different in their marketing, which quite frankly is a form of self-sabotage.

If I had to sum up marketing in five words that you could get every single marketing expert to agree upon, **one of those five words would be *differentiation*.** What is different about you; what is unique? Let's face it: on the surface at least, there's probably nothing especially unique about you or your company—**so you have to create those unique elements that differentiate you from everyone else.** Let me repeat that: You have to *create* the innovation. It doesn't happen by accident. So always remember this: ***There's nothing innovative about you or your company unless and until you create it yourself.***

Assuming that you have an average intelligence and you're fairly normal, then you're creative enough to do this. Creativity is in our very nature; we're all born creative, so don't ever let anyone tell you otherwise. **Creativity is simply your ability to**

look at something that everyone else is looking at, and see it slightly differently. I think that the real secret here is to try to *become* an outsider, even if you're an insider. Now, that's not just a little play on words. I'm not trying to be cute, but I do want you to remember it, and I like the way it sounds. *You've got to become an outsider even if you're an insider.* **That's the real secret to marketing innovation, to separating yourself from the competition.**

So don't hesitate to adopt an outsider mentality so that you can look at your business differently. **Think in concepts, see patterns, examine connections, and look for common denominators.** Look at what everyone else is looking at, and see those things differently. This requires you to pull back a little; there really is such a thing as being so close to the forest that you can't see the trees. I know that's a cliché, and for a good reason: there's a heavy element of truth in it.

Many people have what I call "learned helplessness." They just don't see all their options, partly because they're not being creative enough. They're not adopting that "outsider looking in" mentality. They're not looking for patterns and connections and common denominators. They're not trying to combine different ideas, which is also a very important aspect of creativity. You need to look at ideas almost as if they're pieces of a jigsaw puzzle. It's up to you to find new ways to combine them. **Consider old ideas, things that have worked in the past for you, and try to put them together in new and exciting ways.** Or if you're just getting started, if don't have a lot of experience, look at things that are working for other people.

And I'm not just talking about within your industry—

because to be honest, every industry does tend to have that whole blind-leading-the blind mentality, the marketing incest problem where there's nothing new happening. **Look beyond those limitations for any kind of innovation available, and find ways to implement what you discover within your own industry.** One of the reasons why consultants are paid the big bucks is because they're able to do the things that I'm describing to you here. **They're able to see things you can't, because they're outsiders.** They work with so many different industries that they're able to see the connections, common denominators, and patterns linking them. They have that "outsider looking in" mentality... and you can develop that on your own. **So work at consistently combining ideas; get good at seeing things in a conceptual way. Think about how you can use existing models to power innovation.**

Speaking of that: let me give you a real-world example that's at the top of my mind, a little snapshot, if you will, of how we're practicing this principle. I woke up yesterday morning, which was a Sunday, with several projects weighing on me. I was concerned about a certain promotion we've had going for a few years now. **You know the saying: "If you always do what you've always done, you're always going to get what you've always gotten."** Well, this promotion has been a struggle lately. Every year, we keep it alive and moving forward, and every year, it becomes more difficult to sell it. **We needed something new: that's the bottom line.**

I woke up yesterday morning bothered by all of this; and in the morning is when I do my most creative thinking, when I take a lot of notes, brainstorming on paper, writing things out. **So I**

115

just started jotting out some ideas that were like jigsaw puzzle pieces—different project ideas that have worked for us, or different things that we wanted to redo.

I drink a lot of coffee in the morning, and it was very early, still dark outside. So I got my coffee, then went upstairs and sat in my favorite chair in the dark. Now, that may sound funny to you, but it helps me sometimes to just sit in the dark and drink my coffee. After about four or five cups of coffee, interrupted by bouts of going downstairs to write notes, I sort of tranced out, going into almost a heavy meditative state. During my trance, **I started putting together pieces from successful promotions that we've done in the past.** For example, we have a promotion that we did about six months ago called the Direct Pay System. We tested it, and the early numbers weren't exactly phenomenal, but the customers who got involved absolutely loved it. Because of that, some of my staff have been telling me lately, "We really have to re-examine that promotion and figure it out."

So I started thinking about that promotion. And then I started thinking about classified advertising, and how it's much easier today than it was when we first got into the business 20 some years ago (or even 10 years ago), thanks to the Internet. There are so many agencies and brokers that will place classified ads for you, making the process phenomenally simple. I was thinking about that, thinking about our Direct Pay System, thinking about this one promotion where the sales have been getting more and more difficult to acquire, where we know we have to do something different. That's what sparked my thinking in this case: I was especially concerned about that one promotion. Then I began thinking about this new promotion we're launching, which has what we call a three-tiered affiliate commission structure that makes it really attractive.

At that point I had four or five major pieces of the puzzle, so I kept going upstairs to sit in the dark and drink my coffee; and then I'd go downstairs and take notes. When the sun started coming up, I brought my legal pad upstairs. Now I could see the sun coming through the windows as I was drinking coffee and writing notes. **To make a long story short, by the end of the day yesterday, I actually had a sales letter written to generate leads. I finished it up this morning, put an order form together, and we're going to throw it out there pretty soon.** While we're waiting for leads to come in, we're going to scramble like crazy to put the lead fulfillment together so that we can respond immediately. That's still two weeks or so away, but by then, I'll have the whole lead fulfillment aspect done and in place.

This is a good example of taking different bits and plugging them together to create something new. We still don't know how it's going to work, so we're dealing with an element of speculation. **It has to undergo a lot of testing, probably, but we've created something new out of something old. That's what creativity is all about.** That's what a lot of consultants do, which is why they often charge hundreds of dollars an hour... and it's going to take them a long time just to become familiar enough with your business to help you do something like what I just described.

Of course, once I was done putting my pieces together, I brainstormed it out with Chris Lakey this morning. He came up with a whole bunch of ideas to add to and enhance it; so we'll revise it before we throw it out there and start to test and tweak it. **The point is, you do have to become an outsider, even if you're an insider. You need to become your own consultant, looking at things differently.** The good news is that you're only limited by your imagination... and the bad news is the exact same thing. It's all up to you.

Sometimes, it really does take an outsider to point something out to you. Chris's three-year-old son was born blind in one eye, and has some associated sensory processing issues. Plus he was born in China and spent a couple of years in an orphanage there, and that certainly didn't help. Anyway, Chris says, his son's sensory issues make life interesting. Because of them, he likes to smell things, and he likes to taste things. **He is a sensory-seeking child, which means he seeks out things that his senses can experience.** So if he thinks something's going to smell a certain way or may have a scent to it, he wants to see what it smells like. He wants to see what it tastes like, too. He wants his hands all over things, because he wants to feel what the texture is. Recently he was around a bowl of those starlight mints, the little red-streaked mints that are about an inch in diameter. People keep them around as breath-fresheners. Well, he knows what those are, and he wanted to experience those; but he couldn't have them in that moment.

Chris's wife was a little bit frustrated at her little boy, because he wanted them and was pretty upset when he couldn't have them. It wasn't the right time for him to have them—not that Chris and his wife have a problem with him eating the mints. So this friend of theirs said, "Maybe you could carry around a little bag of those mints or the miniatures—they have some that are about half that size. If you carried around a bag of those, when he was around some and couldn't have them, you could show him that you have some and he could have them later. That way, he doesn't feel like he was unable to have something he was around and could have just taken. He would see that you're offering him the ability to have one, deferred. He just needs to wait just a little bit because the timing isn't right in that moment."

It was a bit of a shock to Chris and his wife that they hadn't thought of that. **It was a simple solution to their problem, and yet it was outside of their ability, apparently, to see in that moment.** So they chuckled to themselves at how silly it was that they hadn't thought of it. Now, of course, they're prepared for similar events should they happen in the future. Hopefully, the next time something like that *does* happens, it'll go more smoothly than it did the last time.

When I was considering this strategy as I prepared to write this section, I immediately thought of that story with Chris's son. I think it's a great illustration of this principle. Chris and his wife were insiders in this story. Their friend is an outsider, someone looking at the situation with fresh eyes, from a slightly different perspective. I think this applies to business quite often. **In many cases, you end up being too close to the situation to see it objectively, to really see anything that's innovative.** When you're looking for a fresh, new way to market your products, or to think about your profit margins, or to trim your overhead, or to do anything that relates to your business—well, you might not be able to see it because you're overwhelmed by everything else.

When you're immersed in it on a day-to-day basis, it's hard for you to get a proper perspective on what you're experiencing, whereas someone else might come in and see things with a fresh set of eyeballs, from a somewhat different perspective. This is one of the reasons why consultants are in high demand. A consultant can come in and, assuming they're trained correctly and they're professional at what they do, at least they've got some insight into your situation. **They *will* look at your business with a fresh set of eyeballs.** They'll be able to see things that you can't see because you're living it day-to-day, while they're looking at it from an outsider's viewpoint.

To get that outsider's viewpoint yourself, you need to find a way to step away from your business and look at things from a different angle. You need to put yourself in the position of a prospect, or at least in the position of a consultant looking at your business, without taking it personally. One of the things you tend to do in your business, because you've made it uniquely you, is that you've made it take on your personality. You bristle at the thought that you might have to change something, since you've made it *you*. So when it comes time to take a critical look, you try not to be too critical—because all the ideas you're tackling are things that *you* set in place.

To move forward effectively, you've got to be able to accept your own criticisms as you consider what you're trying to accomplish—whether you're trying to set new goals, or reach new heights, or find a new way to advertise, or formulate a more effective way to bring in customers. **Whatever you're doing, the ability to look at them from another angle is going to be critical.** When you're too close to the situation and don't make a sincere effort to look at it from an outsider's perspective every once in a while, then you can't objectively do the things you need to do to take your business to the next level. You're stuck in a rut. In most cases, you're just doing things the way you've always done them... and that means you get the same results you've always gotten.

Again, your ability to come up with something fresh, something new, something exciting, something that can take your business to the next level, depends on your ability to see things from a different viewpoint, a different perspective. So take a look at your business from an outsider's viewpoint, maybe get some outsider's opinions on your business, and take all those things into consideration.

All this takes hard work, but the more you do it, the better you get at it. **The worst thing that you can do here is to assume that you're not as creative as you need to be, that you lack the ability to do these things.** Many of us look at people who *can* do these things and become intimidated, because, frankly, there are some super-creative people out there. But what most people fail to realize is that even those super-creative people had to develop their skills and abilities. They weren't born that way. *You* **can develop those skills and abilities within yourself, and therefore become the outsider even if you're an insider, because you have developed that outsider mentality.**

CHAPTER NINE

The <u>easiest thing</u> someone can do is stand on the sidelines and argue for the safe and conservative plan.

❖

It takes a hell of a lot courage to
step out and try new things,
but this is the only way to build
our businesses. *We must be bold!*

The Easiest Thing Isn't Always the Best Thing

The easiest thing that a person can do is to stand on the sidelines and argue for the safe and conservative plan. **It takes a hell of a lot of courage to step up and try new things—but it's the only way to build a business. You've got to be bold, willing to take a chance, willing to fail if it comes to that.** Back in the 16th century, Thomas Fuller said that the first, second, and third most important thing in business is to be bold. It's more true today than ever before, I think.

You've got to take calculated risks. You've got to test all kinds of things, and be open and receptive to all kinds of ideas. We're operating in an over-crowded marketplace that's full of aggressive competition, more so than at any other time in history. As I've emphasized before, I don't say this to be negative; in fact, all that competition is a sincerely positive thing, assuming you choose to look at it that way. It means that there are lots of people in your market, spending lots of money. **Whenever you see a lot of competition, you know that there's a healthy market supporting it. You just have to figure out how to get people to spend that money with you instead of anyone else.** To do that, you've got to differentiate yourself from everyone else. You've got to think differently. **You've got to think *bigger*. You've got to be bold, and take bold action.**

The reason that most people don't want to take bold

action is that they're afraid; it's just that simple. Most will never admit it, of course; they have too much pride. So they cover that fear by thinking that being conservative means they're being smart, and they take great pride in the fact that they're always holding back, because they *do* believe that they're smart.

And every time one of those crazy, wild-eyed entrepreneurs goes out and blows up their company by doing stupid, aggressive things, it just makes them feel safer in their convictions. They feel superior as a result, and believe even more firmly that they're on the right road. But they're not. Again, the marketplace is overcrowded with aggressive marketers who are out there being bold, who *aren't* holding back like the conservatives... so they're gaining ground in the conflict. **And make no mistake: this *is* a conflict.** In some ways, you have to think of business as warfare. In a sense, then, you're the general of your own army. **You're the one who's got to be out there mapping out bold, creative new strategies that will help you continue to kick ass in the marketplace, competing effectively and profitably.**

Now, all this does take great courage and great vision; but still, you've got to make a game out of it, too. Have some fun with it. **Make your moves carefully and wisely, and you'll be surprised at how fun and effective this will all be,** especially if you make the best possible use of direct response marketing.

I realize that I'm using words like "careful" and "calculated" while talking simultaneously about being bold, because here's where those words are synonymous. Usually, when you think of people that are doing really bold things, you think of carelessness. But you don't have to be careless to be bold. **If you're trying bold, innovative ideas on a smaller scale, you can be very, very aggressive without being reckless at all.** You have to stay within the limits of the law and certain ethical concerns, and you don't want to risk bankrupting your company, but you still can be extremely bold. Even if an idea fails completely, you're not sunk.

Incidentally, that fear of failure is why a lot of conservative businesspeople and marketers just won't try new ideas: they're afraid of failing. Fear is the only thing that's holding them back. But why be wed to something as debilitating as fear? **Even without risking everything, you *can* be aggressive.** Even if an idea does fail miserably, you're safe, as long as you're testing small. Sure, it's still going to be a little painful if you're attached to it emotionally as so many of us are. If you're in it with all your heart, you're putting it all on the line; so yes, there will be pain. **But at the same time you're only going to lose a little bit of money, and that's a *smart* way to do it.**

So don't be afraid to be bold. **Test as many of your new, innovative, aggressive ideas as you possibly can. Test them on a small scale,** and you'll never have to be like one of those wild-eyed entrepreneurs who blows their company up. **In fact, you're going to find that some percentage of the bold and innovative ideas you test are going to work phenomenally well.** Ultimately, it's a numbers game—like drilling for oil. You're going to get a lot of dry holes, but eventually, you're going to hit a gusher. It may take 10 or 20 tries, but the money you get from hitting one nice pocket of natural gas or oil can more than make up for all the money that you lose on all those failed tests.

Even if you're not an oil wildcatter, you have to adopt and adapt that same mentality within your business: **test consistently, and be willing to lose a little money here and there. Your market is changing constantly, even though you may not be able to see it.** There are plenty of aggressive competitors out there who are *not* thinking conservatively, people who are always going to muscle their way in and try to take all the money that could and should be yours. **It *is* a war. It's constant, heart-pounding warfare.**

And look: just to let you know, we're practicing what we preach here at M.O.R.E., Inc. As I write this, we're a 22-year-old company, working on year 23—and yet we haven't slowed down, haven't tried to rest on our laurels. That's a recipe for disaster! **No, we're changing direction right now with some of our aggressive testing—because if it works, it's going to account for the *next* 22 years of our company.** And it *is* a new direction for us, a totally new direction. But nonetheless, it lets us use all the skills, abilities, knowledge and experience that we've developed over the past 22 years. **We're not doing entirely new things, but we're definitely reaching a new market in a new way...** and if we're successful, there's our next 22 years, and it could lead to more money than we've ever dreamed possible! That's the dream we're all chasing, every time we decide to be bold and innovative and test a bunch of new ideas.

So I would encourage you to do the same. Anybody can sit on the sidelines; anybody can be a critic. And some critics feel so superior when they see other people try and fail. But as the great Teddy Roosevelt once said, **"It's not the critic that counts, it's the man who's actually in the arena."**

Speaking of quotes, here's an interesting one on taking risks by a guru named Leo Buscaglia: "The person who risks nothing does nothing, has nothing, is nothing and becomes nothing. He may avoid suffering and sorrow, but he simply cannot learn and feel and change and grow and love and live." I thought that was an appropriate quote, because **the easiest thing to do is to avoid risks... but what kind of life are you living if you play it safe all the time?** That's not much of a life in general, and it certainly isn't when you're in business. When you get down to it, the easiest thing to do is to decide never to get into business because, well, getting into business has certain risks. You may not succeed. You might have people laugh at you because you didn't succeed. You might not make all the money you want. You might end up flat broke.

There are all kinds of reasons why you should never, ever start a business, so the easy thing to do is to stand on the sidelines and argue for the safe and conservative plan. You can always put your money in a money market account. It may not be incredibly profitable, but you're not going to lose your money. It's going to sit there and collect the little bit of interest the bank is willing to give you... so it's pretty much safe, until they start charging you fees on it because they can't figure out how to make money any other way in this economy. **The way you make more money is to take some risks;** do the stock market thing, do the mutual funds thing, buy gold, whatever you're doing beyond putting your money in a nice, safe bank account. The easiest thing to do is to take it slow, take it real easy. You'll face very little risk. When you look back on your life and see that you played it safe, though, you'll realize that you have nothing to show for it, either.

On the flip side, it takes a hell of a lot of courage to step out and try new things. But this is the *only* way to build your businesses. You must be bold. You need the courage to move beyond your comfort zone, to go into places where you've never gone before. T.S. Eliot once said, "Only those who risk going too far can possibly find out how far one can go." **If you never experience life out on the edge, how do you know where the edge is?** How can you know how far you can go? If you play it safe all the time, you never know what you might have become, what you could have been.

There's a movie called *Facing the Giants*. It wasn't a big blockbuster hit or anything, but it's a nice little movie about facing and overcoming your fears. In the movie there's a particularly moving scene. It's about a football team, and the coach feels like he's not getting a 100% effort out of his players as they're preparing for their next opponent. In fact, he feels like they're not giving any kind of solid effort at all. So he has them do these drills where the linemen—the bigger, and heavier, and stronger guys—get down on the ground on their hands and their feet, but not their knees. Next, the lighter guys lie down on the heavier players' backs with their feet in the air, so they're back-to-back, basically. The guy on top puts his hands back over his head and holds on to the shoulder pads of the guy on the ground.

So if you can picture this, the one guy is on the ground, on just on his hands and feet—not his knees. The other guy is on his

130

back, back to back, with his feet up in the air a little, his knees above his chest, holding on. The guy on the ground has, say, 150-170 pounds on his back—and he has to crawl along without his knees touching the ground, going as far as he can. These football players are strong, toughened by all kinds of strength conditioning, and so they should be able to go quite a ways, right? But they didn't get that far: some of them made it 10 yards or so. Of course, once they collapse, that's it, the drill is over.

Well, the coach didn't feel like he got enough effort out of them. They were trying... but they were also complaining about how they were going to get slaughtered in this football game that was coming up against a team that was bigger, faster, and stronger than them. He just said, "Guys, I don't feel like you're giving me all that you could be giving. How do you expect to compete Friday night when you aren't even giving me all you've got here in practice?" And then he calls one of his team leaders over, and he gets him down on the ground again and says that he wants him to do it again... except this time, he wants him to give it all he's got. And he wants him to not give up, to just keep pushing through.

He blindfolds the player, because he wants him to be unable to see how far he's gone... **because the fear is that if he _knows_ how far he's gone, he'll be more willing to just give up whenever he feels he's gone far enough.** The coach asks him something like, "Can you give me 30 yards?" And he says, "I think I can." And the coach responds, "No, I want you to give me 30. I want you to give me _50_." I don't recall how the conversation goes, exactly, but he basically says, **"I don't want you to stop. I want you to go as far as you can."** And so the whole drill starts over, and the player gets to the 10 yards that he wanted. You can already tell he's pretty tired, but he keeps going.

He's inching along, he's scooting forward, and of course this guy is on his back, and he keeps pushing. The coach is down on the ground right next to him, just cheering him on, hitting the ground and saying, "One more yard. One more yard," trying to get as much out of him as he can possibly can. This scene seems like it takes forever. He keeps saying, "Just give me one more yard. Keep pushing as far as you can. Don't give up. Don't quit now."

Eventually the player collapses, and the coach takes the blindfold off, and he's gone all 100 yards.

The moral of the story is that the player *wasn't* giving everything he had at first. He didn't even know he'd be able to go 100 yards, because he'd never tried to go anywhere near that. **But by pushing as far as he possibly could, until he physically could not go any farther, he was able to realize how far he *could* go.** He had to push his way through the uncertainty and lack of understanding of his own limits.

I think that's what this strategy is all about. **It's about having the guts that it takes to push through and be bold and go where you didn't even realize that you *can* go.**

There's one more quote that I'll read here, from a gentleman named Andre Malraux, a French historian. He said, "Often the difference between a successful person and a failure is not that one has better abilities or ideas, but the courage that one has to bet on one's ideas, to take a calculated risk—and to act." What Malraux is saying is that it's not about skill, it's not about having better abilities or better ideas, it's not about being smarter— **it's about having the courage to think that you have it all figured out, at least enough to take that calculated risk and to act on it.**

And he *does* say "calculated risk," a point which you should keep in mind. In business, you don't want to take stupid risks. That's like going to Vegas and throwing all your money down on red or black, or odd or even, or whatever. That's taking a foolish risk. It may pay off in the end, but it's just as likely not to. You want to take calculated risks, but you have to take those risks no less. And so as Malraux said, **you've got to be willing to decide that your ideas are at least worth taking a risk on, and to put it all out there, and go as far as you can go, and push yourself beyond your comfort zone until it hurts so bad that you have to quit.**

And sure, that was in a football movie—but you can apply the concept to business, too. You may ask yourself, "What's quitting? How do I push myself until I break?" Well, I don't know what that is for you. It may mean that you "fail" in some fashion; you don't receive the results you were looking for, maybe, or your promotions don't work like you want them to. Hopefully, it doesn't mean bankruptcy and the collapse of your personal economic situation... but in some cases, it might. A lot of successful business people went bankrupt one or more times before they succeeded. Certainly, they had many failures before they failed their way to success, and achieved the results that really set them apart in the industry or made people stand up and take notice. **So it's pushing yourself beyond what you're**

comfortable doing, taking those extra calculated risks to try new things. You've got to do things you've been unable to do before, or push your business into the areas you've never ventured into before. Push the envelope, and see where the results take you.

Again, as T.S. Eliot said, "Only those who risk going too far can possibly find out how far they can go." **Until you've pushed yourself, you never know how far you can go. That's really what this is about.** It's easiest to just stand on the sidelines, play it safe, play it conservative. But the ones who achieve the best results, the ones who break through, are the ones who push the envelope all the way. They push until they break. They push until they can't push anymore, and that sets the new barriers. That's the goal for the next time. So choose. Do you want to sit on the sidelines? **Do you want to play it safe... or do you want to push the envelope and go all out and try to build the best business you can?**

I know the path I've chosen, and it's the path I recommend for you as well. As William Blake said, "The road to excess leads to enlightenment." **As long as you keep pushing yourself, your best is going to continue to get better. As long as you test enough new ideas, you're going to become more innovative.** You're going to keep your company alive as it goes through all its inevitable changes, and you'll stay on top of it all instead of going under like so many other people do. That's the bottom line here.

CHAPTER TEN

Every once
in a while
you should ask
yourself:

"Do I own
a business
or a job?"

Do You Own a Business...
Or a Job?

Every once in a while, you should sit back and ask yourself, "Do I own a business, or do I just own a job?"

So how can you tell the difference? There are a couple of ways. **First of all, can the business run without you being there all the time?** Can the business make it without you? If the answer is "no," then you're probably in trouble. What would happen if you ended up in the hospital for a month or two, flat on your back? What if you were incapable of working? **Could the business continue without you? If not, then you might own a job.** In fact, the answer for so many small business people is, "Absolutely not." Without them in the picture, there *is* no picture.

They try to do everything themselves; they try to wear all the hats in the business. **Now, smart business people are *willing* to do everything, but they don't do everything. They set up their businesses to run without them,** so if they want to take a vacation, they can take a vacation. They don't have to call in three times a day if they don't want to. God forbid they should end up on their back in the hospital for a few months; but if it happens, the business could still run without them. It wouldn't fold just because they were incapacitated. **If that happened, or a terrible, tragic emergency occurred and they were out of commission for a month or two, things could** continue to carry on.

You have to set things up so that it can, potentially, run like that. Think of your business as an investment; rather than just something you do, it's something you own. You try to work on it, not in it; that's a big point. That just means spending a lot of good quality time doing the kinds of things I've talked about in previous Ways. For example, I've told you that I recently sat in the dark early in the morning, drinking coffee, running downstairs and taking notes, then going back upstairs and just thinking. I was thinking as hard as I could think, thinking as deeply as I possibly could, thinking with a purpose—because I had several interconnected ideas, and I was trying various angles that would let me figure out a way to make it all work together. **That's as good an example as any I can describe concerning what it takes to work *on* your business rather than *in* it.**

Also, you should strive to build your business around your model lifestyle, not your lifestyle around your business. That doesn't mean you'll always achieve this goal, but you need to try anyway. **So which things are most important to you? Try to figure out what they are, and build the business around those things.** Successful business people delegate a lot. They put people in place who specialize in certain areas, so that *they* can specialize in the things that make the company the most money—an idea I'll come back to in a little while. They find people who are strong in all the areas they're weak in, good, competent, capable, talented people, and they set things up so they can spend more of their time working on those fewer things that profit the company the most. **Those things tend to fall into**

two areas: marketing and innovation.

Marketing is all the things that you do to attract and retain the largest group of customers for the longest period of time for the most profit possible. Innovation is a part of marketing: it's all of the things you have that are different and unique, that just blow away the people you're trying to do business with.

You've got to win people's business, and that means you need to have lots of time to think. You're not necessarily getting paid by the hour. **The business is with you all the time.** Oftentimes, business owners do work a lot harder than people who own jobs; but a lot of what they do is a cerebral type of work. **They're living with and thinking about the business constantly.** And of course it's a labor of love for them; their hearts and souls are into it. They're not just doing it for money.

For people who have jobs, it's usually about the money and nothing else. I wish that wasn't the case, but it is. My father worked for the government for most of his life, and to him it was *always* about the money. He thought that was what was most important to me too, and he never understood that it wasn't that way at all. **Sure, the money's a part of it, but it isn't the *main* part.** I'm not working for the money—and that's true for most entrepreneurs. **We build our businesses around our lifestyles, and that gives us the kind of freedom and flexibility you can't find with most jobs.**

People who start new businesses often lose track of this fact altogether. What often happens is that a person has a job, and then they decide to turn that job into their own business. For example, if you're an electrician and you work for XYZ Electric Company, you may decide, "Hey, I should be doing this on my own. I don't need them!" So you start ABC Electric Company, and go from having a job to having a business where you're doing the exact same thing. **But what happens a lot of times is that when you had a job, you thought and acted a certain way; and now, even though you're the boss, you** *still* **have that job mentality.** Even if you have employees, they're really only there to help you do your job.

So what usually happens is that you lose sight of the reasons you decided to do your work as a business instead of just a job. Probably your days are longer than ever, and you have fewer days off. You have to rearrange your schedule just to take a vacation. And because you're doing it all on your own, when you do take a vacation, there's no revenue coming in. Oh, you can hire some people to help you; but those people probably can't do the job as well as you can. **All of a sudden, your business becomes an obligation... and stops being fun.**

Instead of handling it that way, you need to approach your business from an entrepreneurial perspective: **that is, you have to realize, at a very basic level, that you** *do* **have a business rather than just a job that you fill.** You succeed or fail based on the strength of your ideas and the systems you put in place—systems intended to make that business run smoothly, to bring in new customers, and to do more business with your existing customers. **When you have a business that's just a job, you end up succeeding or failing based on the limits of your own personal stamina, and you get burn out because you can only do so many jobs a day.** You're tired all the time, and you haven't taken a vacation in three years, and you're sick of this business that's running your life.

An entrepreneur says, "I am an entrepreneur. I have an electrical business and I'm an electrician. I have a team of electricians. This is how we bring in customers, and this is how we operate systems that make everything run smoothly." **You think in a different manner, and that's how you own a business as opposed to a job. You've got systems in place that make everything run smoothly, like a profit machine.** I think that's probably the biggest difference between having a job and having a business.

Now, if you've always been an entrepreneur, you're not necessarily coming from a job into a business in a similar field, so it's a little easier. I think the hardest transition is when you go from having a job to doing that job as your own business, because you do carry that job mentality with you. It's harder to break free from that mentality of, "This is what I do. I'm an electrician, I'm a plumber, I'm a carpenter, I'm a computer geek." In that mentality, whatever you do is your job. When it becomes a business, you tend to maintain that mentality. Conversely, if you get into a business because you see a marketplace that's primed to be mined, *not* because you already have a job in that business, I think it's easier to make that transition. **You can start out with the idea of making your business model work, creating ideas and systems that help you do that.**

So be careful what businesses you choose to get into, but then make sure you maintain and develop that entrepreneurial spirit that dictates your business. **It's more an attitude of**

having control over your business, instead of letting your business control you. As I've said, your business needs to be able to run on autopilot when you're gone, whether you're sick or on vacation. You need to have employers, suppliers, and vendors who can help you maintain your business processes when you're away or indisposed.

Going back to the electrician model, you don't need to be *the* electrician just because you have an electric company. You can be the entrepreneur to the electricians. In this case, you have a team of people doing the electric work, and you're the one running the business. **You can be the entrepreneur without being the one who's stuck in the job. That's the difference, really.** So remember to occasionally stop and ask yourself, "Do I have a job, or do I have a business?" You have to continue to think about your business as a business, and not as a job.

If you can maintain that entrepreneurial spirit, you *will* come out ahead. Make sure your business is never just a job. Always have fun, and never put yourself in a position where you burn out because you're doing the same old things you were doing before—except that now, you've added the pressure of having it be your own company.

CHAPTER ELEVEN

Wisdom from the notorious
takeover artist,
T. Boone Pickens:

❝Business is not life. Life is tragic. Business is fun! It's like a game you play. It's more like playing a game of racquetball than living life.❞

Business Should Be Fun!

This chapter is based on the wisdom of a man who became famous as a corporate takeover artist, although he's certainly much more than that. His name is T. Boone Pickens. He's been quoted as saying, "Business in not life! Life is tragic. Business is fun. It's like a game that you play. It's more like playing racquetball than living life." I love that quote. **The truth is, the greatest entrepreneurs that I've ever met or read about or studied all have a certain looseness about them.** There's a swagger there. Hey, they're working hard; **in fact, they're working *very* hard. But they're also having a lot of fun doing it.**

They're in it all the way. They're putting their hearts into everything they do. **They care very deeply about their companies and the futures of their companies; and yet, it's still more like a game that they're playing.** And look, you *have* to think of it that way. At the time of this writing, I'm in the third quarter of my life. The law of averages say that, at best, I've got one good quarter left in me, and that's about it. And yet, when I last saw T. Boone Pickens on TV, maybe three or four years ago, he was about 76 years old. At that time he was flying high, making more money than he'd ever made before in his entire business career.

They asked him, "T. Boone, what are you doing? You're

making all this money now—why are you still working so hard?" They did a 15-minute overview of his day, and he was surrounded by all these young people, just having the time of his life. He said, "Look, I've lost three or four fortunes in my lifetime, and I'm just now figuring out how to make money." He was just kind of joking and laughing about it, but **what he was really saying is that it was his passion that kept him going. He was in it with all his heart. He was enjoying every moment of it.** Then, of course, a couple of years ago, I read that he lost something like seven billion dollars, which was the bulk of his fortune. So he lost it all again. Oh, he's still a multimillionaire; don't feel too sorry for him. I assume that T. Boone is still alive as I'm writing this, and I'll bet you he has no interest in slowing down. **He's *still* in it with all his heart.**

That's the deal here, so don't take everything so seriously. Have some fun. **You've got to lighten up if you want to become enlightened**—and I really am talking about enlightenment here, because so many business people do take it too seriously. They take *all* their problems too seriously. Years ago, the first time my wife and I went to San Antonio, Texas, we took the little boat cruise in the river that runs through the city. You can see a good portion of downtown San Antonio as you're going through the tour. The tour guide was describing the buildings, and in the case of one building we were passing near, he talked about how in the stock market crash of 1929, all these business people jumped off that building.

So I'm looking at the building and visualizing all these people jumping off it. I've got a pretty good imagination, and that's stayed with me all these years. I was thinking, "Why would somebody take it that seriously?" **Well, since then, I've actually had moments where I *have* taken the business that seriously.** I'm not saying that I was thinking about committing suicide, but I understand the level of depression that you can experience when things go wrong.

Still, you have to get a grip on yourself. Folks, this is just a game that we play. **This is *not* about life and death, and it's not even really tragic. *Life* is tragic.** People dying, becoming deathly ill, wars, tsunamis—those are tragic. That's life. **Business is just a damn good game that you can play; and yes, you can play it with your whole heart and soul.** You can put yourself into it fully. **It can lead to all kinds of personal fulfillment that can spill over into the rest of your life.**

Last Thursday, Chris Lakey talked to me about a project he's working on, for a business that both he and I are involved in. He's been working on it for a few weeks now, and **he pointed out to me that it's a real labor of love. I told him, "Man, that's music to my ears, because that's what it's all about."** It's about getting as much fun and enjoyment out of it as you possibly can, and putting your whole self into it, and it really *does* spill over into all of the other real areas of your real life.

I've had many conversations with people about business and money; and the thing I always come back to in the end is that money is just money. If someone were to take away all your money, your family's still going to be there. Your kids are still going to be there; your parents are still going to be there; your spouse is probably still going to be there. Most of your friends are still going to be there, and those who aren't really aren't your friends anyway. **Those things are the things that are *real*.**

MONEY MACHINE

Money isn't real. It's not even backed by gold anymore. Until our government changes the way we handle the Fed and our currency, a dollar is just a slip of paper that's worth a certain value because the government says it is, and we agree. Until we start trading in real gold and silver and precious metals again, it's just paper.

Businesses come and go. That's not real life. **Real life is all the other stuff you deal with, the valuables that really matter.** Your business can fail, and you can start another business. Your bank accounts could all get drained, but you can fill them up again. **You've only got one shot at life.** You only have one shot at a marriage. You want to maintain good relationships with your family and with your friends. *Those* **are the things that are really important. Businesses come and go; money comes and goes.**

So have fun with it. Who wants a business that you suffer through? You could probably go get a minimum wage job and suffer, if that's what you wanted. If you're into suffering, there are all kinds of boring, tedious jobs you could happily hate. **But you don't get into a business to hate! Don't create a business for yourself that's no fun.** *Enjoy* **your business life.** Enjoy the game, the hunt, and the challenge that comes along with building something and trying to innovate and create profits and serve a marketplace. **Enjoy the challenge of getting people to decide that they like what you have enough to give you their money in exchange for it.**

Of course, you need money to live. I'm not suggesting that you should go broke and live life on the streets, or hole up on a little farm and eat out of your garden while surviving

148

without power and running water. **You need *some* money, but don't take the process of acquiring it too seriously.** There are *all kinds* of ways to acquire money legally. **There are all kinds of things you can do and have fun doing.** So as you think about business, and as you think about what you want to do with your life economically, think about the things that bring you pleasure. Think about the things that allow you to have fun.

Now, you need to run this idea that your business can be fun up against a viable business model. You could have fun in an industry where there's zero profit, so that's not necessarily a good match. **But if you find a marketplace that you can serve and it happens to be something that's fun, then you're golden.** If it's a field you're interested in or excited about, then all the better for you. You can have fun, and you can make money. You can serve a marketplace that you're excited about. It all leads to an enjoyable life and profits that put food on the table and cars in the driveway.

That's what T. Boone Pickens was talking about. Business isn't life. Your life is your life. **Life is tragic; life is full of drama enough on its own.** Business should be fun, and you need to make your business fun for you. If you'll keep that strategy in mind, you'll enjoy it a lot more. **You'll seek things out that bring you pleasure in your business life. You'll avoid things that don't.** Opportunities will present themselves for you to have fun and make money.

I think that's what Pickens was talking about with this quote. It's a good one.

CHAPTER TWELVE

★★★

We are <u>all</u> self-made... but only the successful will admit it.

Ultimately, We Are All Self-Made

There's a funny little quote I heard a long time ago that states, "We're all self-made, but only the successful will admit it." Most people never figure this one out; or maybe they do, and just won't let themselves see it. You see, almost everybody's out there making excuses for why they don't succeed. **But if you really want to get good at making money, you have to let all of the excuses go.** Because let's get real: **people who make a lot of money and become successful in business have more opportunities for making excuses than anybody.** They deal with more problems, pain, aggravation, and setbacks in a year than most people deal with in a lifetime.

Again, I'm not trying to be negative or dissuade you from pursuing success. **But the harsh truth is that the more money you want to make, the more problems you're going to face.** That's only common sense. Don't believe the lies that people spread, the lies that say you can make millions of dollars without having millions of dollars worth of headaches. It just doesn't happen. **You've got to take total responsibility for your own success... or failure.** Remember, people who are great at making excuses are lousy at making money.

A while back, I read about a very successful business consultant named Mary Parker Follet, one of the very first female consultants, who pointed out, **"Responsibility is the**

great developer of men." The more you're responsible for, the more you take upon your shoulders, the more problems you're going to have—but you're also going to have more opportunities to develop yourself as well. **And that's what being self-made is all about: developing yourself.** It's about becoming all you can be, just like the Army used to advertise in its commercials. Just be all you can be, developing yourself fully.

You don't do that in a vacuum. **You do it by going through all kinds of pain, problems, adversities, frustrations, and setbacks, and developing your skills along the way.** That's how you maximize your potential. It's all about developing skills... and that takes work, unfortunately.

Everybody's looking for an easier, softer way. Everybody wants all the good stuff without having any of the bad. **Everybody wants all the results without paying the price.** To use a metaphor, everybody wants the great body, but they don't want to go to the gym. They don't want to watch their calories or do any the other stuff that's necessary to get one of those hard bodies. Well, it's the same way with business and making money. **People want to make millions of dollars... but they just don't want to do what's necessary.**

You don't have to look at this as a bad thing. In fact, I think it can be a damned good thing. **There's more room for you to accomplish your goals, since no one else is willing to try very hard.** If you want to make a lot of money, you're going to have to pay a large price to get that. Accept that. The more money you want to make, the bigger the price you're going to have to pay. If I'm the first person telling you this, then that's a shame— because I know that there are a lot of people who promise instant money.

And maybe some people who want to make millions don't really *need* millions. Thirty years ago, when I first got this insatiable ambition to make millions of dollars, that's all I thought about. I just wanted to be a millionaire. Now, all that I knew about millionaires was the crap I saw on TV and in the movies. Hell, I didn't even know what a millionaire *was*—I just knew I wanted to be one. **Since then, I have discovered that... Well, let's just say that life is like the Beetles song from the early 1960s, "Can't Buy Me Love." Money doesn't buy love, and it doesn't buy you a lot of other things either.**

Part of my insatiable desire for millions of dollars was a bit delusional, and I think that a lot of other people are just like I was then. They *think* that they want to make millions and millions of dollars, but they're unwilling to do what it takes to make that money, because they really don't *need* millions of dollars. **I think that they could make their lives a lot easier by setting smaller goals rather than larger ones. The smaller goals are more easily achieved; and then, if they want to make more money after they achieve those smaller goals, they can move forward.**

Back when I first got this insatiable ambition to get rich, I was very envious of people who lived in big houses and drove nice cars and took big vacations and had "all the good things of life." I had a big chip on my shoulder about it, so I was running around frustrated and angry all the time. I was like a ticking time bomb. I remember this one time when I was going on and on about all these rich people who had it so much better than me. I was doing this in front of a good friend of mine, and she listened to me for maybe 10 or 15 minutes. Then, finally, she just had enough. She basically started screaming and yelling at me.

Now, at that time, I was living in a government-assisted apartment. Adjoining this apartment that I lived in, there was a really nice neighborhood, and I used to walk through that neighborhood at nighttime. So my friend told me, "Look! Just go up to anyone of those houses, knock on the door, and ask them what they had to do to get their money!" Well, if I'd done that, they might have called the cops on me; she was just using that as an example. **But basically, she told me what I'm telling you now: most of those people had to pay a tremendous price to get what they've gotten in life.** At the time, I was in my very early 20s; I was young and dumb and I really didn't get it. And I think a lot of people that age—and older—still don't get it. **They're envious of people who've achieved a certain level of success, forgetting the price altogether.**

Those people who have reached that height of inner mastery and performance, who have honed their ability to do all these wonderful things—including making money—**well, they sometimes make it look easy.** Maybe it looks from the outside like they were blessed with some special ability, so they didn't have to work their asses off to achieve what they have. And sure, that may happen sometimes. But having now read hundreds of biographies of successful people, and having come to know almost as many, I can tell you that nearly all of them had to pay a tremendous price to get where they are.

You can get there, too. If you're like me, and you're unwavering in your determination to make as much money as you can, then you can make however much you want. But know

156

that you *are* going to have to pay a price for it. Again, I'm not trying to say that in a negative way, to put you off. It's just a truth you have to face. **All super-successful people are self-made, and they got that way by paying the price required.**

I will say this: the bigger your goals are, the more driven and determined you're going to be. So set some goals. They don't have to be big in the monetary sense; just big in terms of what you really want to accomplish. I've got such a goal hanging on my wall right now, right in front of one of the treadmills where I do my walking in the morning. This is a little sign I wrote to myself. **Basically, I want our company, M.O.R.E., Inc., to be the first information marketing company to dominate the mainstream network marketing industry.**

The network marketing industry has been around since the 1940s; it's a multibillion dollar industry. There are huge corporations that are a part of this market, and I believe that information is the greatest product ever. But information is intangible in nature, and trying to market information products represents some unique challenges. **No company, to the best of my knowledge, has ever really dominated the market of selling information to the mainstream network marketing industry.**

So in my determination to achieve this goal, my willingness to do whatever it takes, we have two separate projects that we're working on right this minute. We're putting a lot of time, work, effort, energy and money, and all the resources that we have at our disposal, into these things. We're working very hard, burning the midnight oil, putting in tons of extra hours—working harder than most people can understand.

Because let's be honest here: most people are employees, as I discussed in the previous way. They want to work 9 to 5, and that's basically it. **A lot of small business people are the same way; they're trying to get by with the minimum effort possible, not really pushing themselves as hard as they could.** They may think that they're working hard, but they're really not. They lack the necessary focus, drive, and determination to really give it all they've got. They're just not putting their entire selves into the effort. They're coasting.

I don't want to claim that I've never done that myself; I struggle with this tendency, too. **But I will say this: the more I stay focused on my goals, maintaining goals that interest me and make me determined, the harder I work.** And it's just that simple. There are a million books on goal setting... and you can throw them all away. You don't have to read any of them to know that **when you find something you can get passionate about, you'll be willing to put an amazing amount of effort into it.**

Just sit down, and write it all out so that it's very clear to you. **Keep that goal in front of you, so you keep thinking about it all the time. Start working on projects that will allow you to reach that goal.** That's the only way I know to truly become self-made.

You have to realize that this is one of those Ways that's more conceptual than many of the others in this book. In one sense, there's not a whole lot more to be said about it; in a more conceptual sense, though, you can talk about it for hours—and I've certainly spent a good bit of time on it. It all starts with that initial quote at the beginning: "We're all self-made, but only the successful will admit it." *We are all self-made*, whether we're willing to admit it or not. **No matter what stage of life you find yourself in, whatever your socioeconomic class or income scale or quality of life, there's a good chance that it's mostly your own doing.** For many people, that's not an easy thing to hear; and yet it's mostly true, at least here in the United States.

You could argue that different countries have different situations, and that may be true. If you live in certain countries in Africa, Asia, or South America, you may be mired in extreme poverty and disease. A child in some parts of Africa, for example, has a good chance of growing up without a mom or a dad because they died of AIDS, and their situation is grim—so yes, they've got very little chance of getting out of that situation. But we're not talking about kids here. Adults mostly make their own way.

In any case, the United States was founded on a cherished notion of freedom. **The implementation of it has been far from perfect, but we've gone forward with the idea that if we could only maintain freedom as a basic right, then people would have the ability, to a large degree, to control their own destinies and opportunities.** So because of the freedom that we enjoy here, this principle, this is true in a sense that it might not be elsewhere. You have the freedom to move, the freedom to choose your career, the freedom to pursue your own concept of happiness, at least within certain broad guidelines. There are probably people reading this now who live in states or cities where the economy is doing poorly; and I have to wonder why anyone in business would subject themselves to some of the situations I've seen. Now, I understand the love of a particular area, and a desire to stay near family; but if you can't succeed where you are, then it may be time to go elsewhere.

Take Detroit. For years, Detroit has been suffering economically, with high unemployment running rampant. I've seen video clips of some parts of that city that look like a ghost town. Huge commercial areas are uninhabited, and the buildings are so dilapidated that they look like you could touch them and they'd fall over. In the U.S., if you live in a city like that, I would think you might want to bolt—take the fast train out of town and get yourself to a place that has more opportunities, where you've got at least a better chance to succeed than you do in a town like that. This was what drove people west and north during the Dust Bowl and the Depression, and why some of these cities grew as big as they did in the first place.

We have the opportunity to do literally what we want, within certain moral and legal bounds. Sure, there are some silly laws constraining us; but mostly, people can operate under a certain banner of freedom. **That allows us to make choices for ourselves that can either improve our lot in life... or take us down a notch.** If I decided not to work anymore and I just wanted to stay home and eat potato chips and watch TV, well, I soon wouldn't have the ability to watch TV, because they'd take away my cable... though I guess I could always watch the broadcast networks if I had a good antenna.

My cell phones would all be taken away, though. The utilities would be cut off. Eventually I would have nothing... and maybe that could be my lot in life, and I could be happy just not having much. But then I'd get my house taken away. I could probably manage to find a place to live, maybe in a homeless shelter, and I could get something to eat in a soup kitchen or something. So yes, I could get enough food and shelter to at least survive, but I wouldn't have much beyond that. That would be my choice, though.

On the flipside of that, you also have the ability to succeed, even if you start out poor... although I don't know that anybody is truly poor in the United States. The poor here live much better than 99% of the people in the rest of the world. **Nonetheless, let's say you're poor by American standards, and you have an idea. There's nothing that prevents you from finding a way to make that idea come to fruition in the marketplace.** There's nothing keeping you from taking that idea and becoming successful with it.

You have the ability to publicize your idea, even if you're poor, if you're ingenious enough. There was a story a while back that you might remember. A gentleman who was homeless ended up being seen on TV. He had one of those deep, resonant announcer-type voices; when you listened to him, he sounded like he belonged on the radio or on television. He didn't look like the kind of person that his voice sounded like—not at all—but his voice was perfect for that kind of thing. You wondered how a person like that could end up being unemployed and homeless; yet there he was on the street, begging for money with a sign.

A local TV station saw him and asked him to talk, because his sign said that he had a voice from God, or like God, or something like that. They were curious, so they had him talk on camera, and this clip made it onto YouTube and he amazed people. Within just a couple of days, this YouTube video had millions of hits! All of a sudden he had job offers from the NBA and MSNBC to do commentary. Several big companies had seen the video and were interested because of all the publicity.

Well, it turns out that this gentleman, through his own doing, had gotten involved in drugs and alcohol, and had taken a downward spiral and lost the job he had—again, because of his own decisions. He was trying to get straight, and had been clean for two years when the YouTube video was made. **He was just looking for another break, and ended up getting one.** As I'm writing this, it's not clear where he'll end up. **He's had some problems and difficulties; and remember, this is a gentleman who, through his own doing, was down.** And you could say it wasn't his own doing that he was discovered. And yet, he was out there holding a sign talking about how he had a voice like God, and someone discovered him and had him talk. Once that video clip made its way to YouTube, the rest, as they say, is history.

The concept of being self-made really just means that it's up to you to decide what you're going to do and who you're going to become. To a large extent, your success or failure will have much more to do with your own determination than luck, or happenstance, or what other people do to you, or the circumstances you may find yourself in. Because people do succeed in all walks of life. It's not just the "educated" people who succeed, or those born into wealthy families. It's not just people who were lucky and won the lottery. The success stories written up in business books aren't always about the well-off. A lot of times, those success stories begin with people who are stuck in hard places, whose lives weren't handed to them on silver platters; **and yet they choose to do what it takes to be successful, and to refuse to ever give up.**

Sure, there are other factors that go into success. **Sometimes overnight successes are really 20-year success stories in the making.** But these kinds of things rarely happen because you're sitting at home moping over your present life situation. **They usually happen because you decide that you're going to do whatever it takes to succeed. That's how we become self–made.** Whether you succeed or not, it's mostly at your own hand. That's an unpopular message for many people, because any unsuccessful person will give you a million reasons why they're unsuccessful. They've bought into all of their excuses, and they have a lot of them. **That's why I say that we're all self–made, but only the successful will admit it: because they're the ones who paid the price, took the action, and then suffered all of the consequences, both good and bad, along the way.**

CHAPTER THIRTEEN

When you say, "YES!" to one thing and totally put your heart into it — you are automatically saying "No!" to many other things.

Be Careful What You Say "Yes" To

A basic fact of the business life—indeed, a basic fact of life in general—is that **when you say "yes"" to one thing, you automatically say "no" to many other things.** This is a corollary to the whole idea of staying focused and putting your whole heart and soul into something, a concept I'm totally in tune with. Vincent Van Gogh, the great artist, once said, "I am seeking, I am striving, and I am in it with all my heart."

If you study Van Gogh's biography, you'll see that he was definitely in it with all of his heart. His passion ruled everything for him. **When people are moving forward in the direction of their dreams, it absorbs them; they don't have a whole lot of time for a whole lot of other things.** They become very focused. In one of his poems, Robert Browning points out, "Less is more." This is easy to see, because **people who are very, very focused in some ways often live very simple lives otherwise, because they're so focused on what they're putting their heart and soul into that they don't have time for anything else.** By saying "yes" to those things, they automatically say "no" to a lot of other things. It's one of the keys to their success.

Here's a simple way of explaining that in my own life. I'm very, very focused on the same thing most entrepreneurs are focused on: "How do we serve our customers better? How do we sell more stuff to them, and how do we attract those people in the marketplace whom we haven't done business with yet?" **I'm saying yes to all the ways of serving my customers and prospects, reselling them additional items related to the products and services they bought the first time.** I'm always thinking about them, what turns them on, and what's going to work the best and make them the happiest, so they'll keep coming back to buy more.

By moving in that one direction, it's easy for me to stay away from all these other things. And there *have* been times in my life, just in the last decade for example, when I wanted to do something different. There was one time in particular that I wanted to get involved with a certain group of people; I had an interesting way of selling some stuff to their customers, and it would have represented an entirely new business for me... but when I presented this to them they said, "No." At the time I was a little bit heartbroken and upset. Now I look back at it and say, "Hey, that was the greatest thing ever. I am so grateful that they said 'no,' because I would have gotten too involved in a whole lot of things had they said 'yes' to me." **Now I can see things there that I wouldn't want.** It would have created many, many problems, because a partnership with those people wouldn't have been good for me or for them. We would have driven each other crazy.

And other times, I've almost gotten into certain businesses and I've backed off because I just couldn't figure out a way to sell them to my customers; **I couldn't find a way to take my customers with me, so to speak. Because I'm focused on that one direction, it makes decision making become easier.**

Now, let me go off on a related tangent here for a moment.

A lot of our clients are plagued with this one question that's just driving them nuts: "What products and services should I sell?" They're too focused on that. Admittedly, it's an important question, but we tell them that the important thing is to build the customer base and get rich by reselling to their customers again and again. It's as simple as that; with some rare exceptions, that's how all fortunes are built. We tell our customers, **"Once you have your own client base of people that you're dedicated and committed to, and you really want to serve them, the decisions about what to sell become much, much easier."** Once you narrow your focus to what they want, you eliminate a whole lot of choices—and that's always a good thing.

I know some people in business who... well, let's just say that they like to play more than they like to work. One friend of mine in particular loves to play a lot, and he'll admit it, too. He's got all these different interests he's involved in. He *says* that he wants to make money, but his actions suggest otherwise. **All his diversions take him away from his moneymaking efforts; and in all the years that I've known him, he's never made any significant amount of money because of his lack of focus.** He does stay extremely active, I'll give him that. But by saying "yes" to all these different things that he's involved with, he's saying "no" to making a lot of money. That's not a judgment call; it's just an observation. For the most part he's a happy guy, and he's got a lot of things that interest him. But he says he wants to make a lot of money, and as I've discussed before, that requires sacrifice, dedication, commitment, discipline, and focus.

By saying "yes" to one thing, you automatically say "no" to a lot of other things. That's just the way it is, and maybe the reverse is true, too—that is, by saying "no" to something, you're automatically saying "yes" to something else. **I think this really boils down to scheduling and commitments.** The fact that you say "yes" to one thing automatically determines that you *have* to say "no" to at least one and maybe several other things. I suppose you can take it to an extreme: **the more things that you say "yes" to, the more things you're saying "no" to. To some degree this is about time management.** The reality is that we all have the same 24 hours a day in our schedule; and we all sleep for some of that time. Yes, some of us get by on five hours of sleep and some of us take 10. But generally, that limits our accomplishments to the waking hours. Even then, there are certain basic things that have to be done just about every day: showering, brushing your teeth, combing your hair, getting dressed, eating, using the restroom. That leaves a chunk of time in everybody's day that can only be divvied up so many different ways.

Just think about the things that you could do with your day. Most of us like to watch TV in some fashion or another. Maybe we're into sports, and we'll take three hours on a Sunday afternoon to watch a football game, or maybe six hours if we watch both the noon and the 3:00 o'clock games. Well, there's an evening game too, so on Sunday, you can blow nine hours watching all three games that are on TV that day. Add a couple of hours for pre–game stuff in the morning and a couple of hours afterward for the post, the reviews and analysis, and you can basically blow all day watching football on a Sunday.

Similarly, if you're a big TV fan, and every evening you're sitting down from seven to ten o'clock watching all the TV to be had, then those "yeses" mean that you're saying "no" to other things that could be more productive. **Saying "yes" to 10 hours of television in a week means saying "no" to 10 hours of productivity in your business.** I'm not saying that TV is necessarily bad, but it's inherently less productive than most business activities. **So it's a time balance issue.** You're choosing what to say "yes" to, and by default saying "no" to other things. Similarly, saying "yes" to cake on a regular basis means that you're saying "no" to good health. Now, you could eat cake *and* exercise, although that's probably not going to be very productive either. **So in general, you have to choose carefully what you are saying "yes" to and what you're saying "no" to.**

In the area of business and productivity, saying "yes" to your business means that you're committing yourself to what it takes to be successful. You set your day up for maximum productivity. You don't watch as much TV, because you need to work on your business. You set aside time each day to work on advertising. You don't lounge around or sleep late, or do any number of other things that would impact your productivity.

By being committed to your business, you have to say "no" to other things that would get in the way of your success. **You can't be half-committed to your business and have other things take a priority, and then question why your business isn't as successful as it could be.** So saying "yes" means saying "no," in the sense that you're prioritizing your commitments. If you're committed to being a couch potato, then you can say "yes" to doing that and you can say "no" to other things. **I think that, by nature, "yes" is a single commitment and "nos" are**

multiple, in the sense that the strategy of saying "yes" to one opportunity makes you say "no" to at least several others. If you're committed to maintaining good fitness, for example, that's a single "yes"; so if you're constantly invited to parties where people are eating tons of unhealthy foods, you have to make a conscious effort to say "no" to all the many opportunities you have to eat unhealthy food. **If you've committed to being successful in business, that means you have to say "no" to a lot of different things that may fight for your time and attention.**

If you say "yes" all the time, then you won't be good or committed to anything. Though if you say "no" all the time, well, you never do anything either. So you have to balance your commitments properly: you have to choose very carefully what you say "yes" to and choose what you say "no" to. **Those two things weigh against each other in most of the things you do, so be careful in your choices.** As you get better at this, you'll find time management coming easier, because you've balanced your priorities and you're committed to the things that are most important to you.

The uncommitted life isn't worth living, you see. By committing yourself to your business and a few other things that are most important to you, you're automatically saying "no" to a whole lot of other things that don't involve those few things you're deeply committed to. **You're living a very disciplined, focused kind of life; and as long as it's something that has meaning to you, then it can be a life of bliss.** A lot of successful people are living those kinds of lives. They enjoy what they do, and they're good at it.